# DOWN
## THROUGH THE
# YEARS

# *Applause* for Jean Shepherd

Jean was one of the first *Grand Ole Opry* people that I ever really felt like I got to know on a personal level long before I came to the *Opry*. She is the first *Opry* artist that I ever interviewed in my disc jockey days.

Of course, there's the legendary story about me not knowing when to cut off the interview. Finally, Jean was so nice to me, she said, "Well, Bill, I've taken up enough of your time." But it was just the opposite, I'd taken up too much of her time!!

I love Jean. I love touring with her. I love being out on the road with her and Benny. Because number one, you never know what to expect! And number two, you know you're going to laugh. Jean is such a wonderfully warm, funny, and caring person. I just can't think of anybody that I love any more.

—BILL ANDERSON, *Grand Ole Opry* Star

What I always loved about Miss Jean is that she always treated me like an equal. She treated me like a family member before they inducted me out here (at the *Grand Ole Opry*). Then, when I found out that she was an Okie, it all made sense. She's just a doll inside and out, and that's what I love about her.

—GARTH BROOKS, *Grand Ole Opry* Star

I think that Jean Shepard, as the matriarch at the *Grand Ole Opry*, is pretty amazing for the many years she has been singing here. I think she's a little overlooked and a little bit underrated by a lot of people. I really value her contributions to this place and to this music. I love the fact that she is an Okie and she makes the best sausage balls–better than anybody at the *Grand Ole Opry*.

—VINCE GILL, *Grand Ole Opry* Star

There is one lady at the *Grand Ole Opry* that I've always admired because she never hit a flat note; she never hit a sharp note; but she could sing just about any song that she wanted to sing. She could go anywhere from pop to country. She's here because she loves country and I sure am glad that she is. Jean Shepard is truly one of those great ladies that everybody loves. What can you say about somebody who is beautiful, a great singer, and a great person?

—JIM ED BROWN, *Grand Ole Opry* Star


I have a lot of respect for Jean Shepard. She is a crusader. I've got a thing about crusaders, patriots, and people who fight for a cause. She has always stood up for traditional country music. She will tell you in a minute that's where it's at for her. It's the real thing—real country music. She is a partisan. I think folks will know what I mean. She is one of the great crusaders for traditional country and we have to hang onto that or we will lose that tradition. Eddie Stubbs told me that Jean has been on the "*Grand Ole Opry*" longer than anybody. She joined it some years ago, and she never left. Some of us have come and gone a couple times. A lot of the *Opry* members who started back in that era left for a while for one reason or another and did other things. But Jean Shepard has been here since 1955, so she is now the artist with the longest tenure. Although she is a young gal, she is the senior member because she has been here the longest. I'd just like to say, may she *Stay Forever Young*. I love you, Jean, think the world of you, and am proud of you for standing up for real country music and keeping the tradition alive. God Bless You!

—GEORGE HAMILTON IV, *Grand Ole Opry* Star


You know, I've been listening to Jean Shepard for a long time. When she had her hit song, *Dear John Letter*—well, I've been a fan ever since. She is such a great singer, and sings now just as good as she ever did.

—DEL McCOURY, *Grand Ole Opry* Star


I have known Jean Shepard for a lot of years. She came here in 1955 and I came in 1956. We toured the Northwest together that following winter with her and Hawkshaw Hawkins. We went through a lot and had all kinds of experiences. We have been friends ever since. All through the years, she has had so many hits. She is an *Opry* natural and a pioneer in country music. She is a wonderful lady. She is the real deal.

—JIMMY C. NEWMAN, *Grand Ole Opry* Star

Jean Shepard is one of my heroes. I joined a talent contest in Columbus, Ohio, at *Frontier Ranch* where I first met Bill Anderson. He heard me and brought me to Nashville. So I sang *I Thought of You*, one of Jean Shepard's songs. She got me started in the business. So it's all her fault! I love her very much.

—CONNIE SMITH, *Grand Ole Opry* Star

At my house, Connie and I talk about Jean Shepard a lot. We have so much respect for her; we honor her. She really laid so much track for so many other ladies to travel on. When she started, there were no rules; she helped form them. Down through the years, she's just been an essential. I love her dearly. She offered me a job one time, and I had to go to work elsewhere because she worked too much, that was the problem: I was lazy and she wasn't. I've always loved her for that. We love her and Benny very much. The world wouldn't be the same without Jean Shepard.

—MARTY STUART, *Grand Ole Opry* Star

I was in Okinawa in 1953 when the record, *"Dear John Letter"* by Jean Shepard and Ferlin Husky came out. I bought it at the PX and thought it was one of the greatest songs, especially for the GIs. I was in the Air Force as a baker. I served my country by serving cookies and cakes and pies. But I loved that song; and then she came out to perform for us, with some others. She got to yodeling, and I said, "Boy, can that little girl sing!" After I got out of the Air Force, I came to Nashville and have been a fan ever since. I think she is a wonderful lady and a wonderful entertainer.

—MEL TILLIS, *Grand Ole Opry* Star

I have known Jean Shepard since the early '50s. I went to work for Hawk and Jean in 1957. We traveled all over this country and had a great time. Jean was really a great person to work with, and people loved her everywhere we went. She and Hawkshaw made a great team back in those days. I was only 20 years old when I started working for them. They taught me to drive the bus, which probably gave them some gray hairs. I worked for them until Hawkshaw died in the plane crash. I started getting off the road, and I really missed traveling with her. Good luck on this book, Jean.

—EARL WHITE, *Grand Ole Opry* Staff Band Fiddle Player

I just love Jean Shepard. She is one of my favorites. One of the things I like about her is that she is a wonderful person, and so down to earth and "tells it like it is."

—SALLY SMITH *Grand Ole Opry* Green Room - Backstage

# DEDICATION

I would like to dedicate this book to my Mother and Daddy and all of my family. Without their love and support, I would not be where I am today.

# FOREWORD

In the days before large air-conditioned performing arenas and concert halls, venues for country music performers were anywhere and anything. Honky-tonks, school gymnasiums, town squares and flatbed trucks were the order of the day. Two-lane roads, cramped cars with bass fiddles strapped on top and trailers dragging behind; bound for anywhere, USA, but mostly the South and rural America. This was reality in country music in the 1950s and 1960s.

These were the days of fast-talking shyster promoters who would manipulate and cheat young performers in a fledgling industry, then disappear with the profits. These were tough times for country music singers, especially those new to the business. These were the cornerstone years of what country music is today, and those who rose to the top during this time were tough, determined individuals with a heartfelt love for their music and their fans.

And out of this cutthroat, male-dominated scene emerged a wide-eyed teenage girl from Paul's Valley, Oklahoma, with a yodel and a dream. Her name: Jean Shepard.

Through hard work, faith, and the help of many, Jean became a real success story. Over 50 years a star on the "Grand Ole Opry," she is now a country music icon and one of the best loved and most respected individuals in the industry.

True, Jean Shepard overcame the pitfalls and challenges of the formative years of country music, but this is not her greatest achievement. This is a lady anyone would be proud for one of their children to look up to as a role model. What higher compliment can any person be paid?

In facing the many trials, triumphs, and tragedies of life, both personal and professional, Jean Shepard never lost faith. She has faith in herself, faith in her family, and most importantly, faith in God. This is her strength.

Though the landscape of country music has changed dramatically through the years, Jean Shepard hasn't changed her approach at all. She never compromised herself, her music, or her ethics, and for this, she is admired, respected, and revered by her fans and peers. This is an extraordinary accomplishment in any walk of life, but especially so in the entertainment business.

Listen to a Jean Shepard recording from any decade of her career and you get tradition. Steel guitars and fiddles are still the focus of her musical message, just as they were when she took the stage of the Opry for the first time. "I chose to stick with what brung me," Jean says. That's Jean Shepard, true to herself, true to her fans, and true to her country music roots.

This also says it all about her character. In over six decades in the business, Jean has never lessened her standards in any way to conform to the whims of a volatile and fickle country music industry. She has risen to the top by focusing on values and ethics; and, though human like all of us, she has tried to live by setting the example. This is the greatest testament to life anyone could ask for.

As you read this account of her path through life, you will realize there is far more to Jean Shepard than being a big star. People like Jean Shepard – the person, the mother, the wife, and the friend – are the rarest, most beloved individuals humanity has to offer. If you don't believe me, ask anyone who knows her.

—Former US Senator Steve Faris, Arkansas

Jean Shepard broke the mold when she stepped onto the country music scene, and more than 60 years later she still stands apart.

It's hard for me to imagine a time when women weren't a big part of country music, but that's the world Jean found herself in. She was a teenager in the early 1950s when she met Hank Williams, who was appearing near her home in California. Since 10th grade Jean had been singing and playing bass in a five-piece act called the Melody Ranch Girls, and she told Williams she was going to be a star.

"There ain't many females in country music," Williams told her.

"Well I'm fixing to change that!" Jean said.

Sure enough, in 1953, the year she turned 20 years old, Jean became the first female country artist since World War II to have a million-selling record. Two years later, the Grand Ole Opry invited Jean to become a member.

In 1955, the year Jean joined the Opry, the Ralston Purina Company sponsored the first Purina "Grand Ole Opry" television shows. Purina had a good product and they knew how to sell. The company was bigger than the next five commercial food manufacturers put together. So the partnership with the Opry was a natural fit – quality and salesmanship on both sides.

Also, by that time my family had been selling Purina feed for nearly twenty-five years, and my father and uncle were Purina's largest customer in the world. So you can imagine that, like thousands of children across the country, I grew up watching the Purina "Grand Ole Opry" with my Daddy. The difference was, come Monday morning, my daddy would sell more feed because of the Opry.

Now fast-forward nearly fifty years. Our company, Springer Mountain Farms, has introduced antibiotic-free chicken in grocery stores, and I'm thinking about doing some advertising. What better place than the Opry? After all, it worked for Purina; and country music and fried chicken go hand-in-hand. And who better to sell our product from the stage of the Ryman than Jean Shepard?

Jean, you need to understand, is the real deal. She believes in the pure country sound. When country music was changing – updating – in the 1970s, she held her ground. She didn't roll with the crowd. Yet she's always working to improve, never resting on her laurels. Today, this Grand Lady of the Grand Ole Opry is still breaking the mold by remaining true to the roots of country music.

Jean Shepard also remains true to her friends, and I am blessed to be one of them. She's also my role model – a model of success, hard work, and loyalty. You can see those traits on every page of her life as you read her book, from her earliest years in the Dust Bowl of Oklahoma, to her growing up years in California, to her six decades as a county music star.

She's a great entertainer with an entertaining and compelling story.

—Gus Arrendale, President, Springer Mountain Farms

Throughout the history of country music, there have been forerunners and those whose work opened doors for others to follow. One of these individuals is Jean Shepard.

Her rise to fame in life and in country music was not an easy journey by any means. Born in the Great Depression to a sharecropping family, she had many a rough row to hoe. Jean has often commented about country music star Loretta Lynn's stories of growing up poor, "Loretta couldn't even spell the word compared to how poor we were."

Jean eventually found her calling in the music business and became the bass player in an all-female group, the Melody Ranch Girls. A chance meeting with country star Hank Thompson facilitated her obtaining a recording contract with Capitol Records in Hollywood in 1952 while she was still a teenager.

In 1952, you could just about count on two hands the number of female artists recording country music. Every one of them – Kitty Wells, Rose Maddox, Rose Lee Maphis, Ramona Jones, Wilma Lee Cooper, Chickie Williams, Goldie Hill, Betty Cody, among others – were all working in a family group with either their husband or siblings.

Destined to make a difference and a name for herself, Jean Shepard, then just 18, was going it alone.

What country music fans and historians often overlook is Jean's involvement and importance to West Coast country music, and specifically to Bakersfield. In fact, one of the later proponents of Bakersfield music, Buck Owens, played electric lead guitar on many of Jean Shepard's recordings several years before he became a well known star.

A Shepard session with Ferlin Husky doing the narration on "A Dear John Letter" in 1953 catapulted the duo into stardom. The number-one country recording and top-five pop hit made Jean Shepard the first female artist in post-World War II country music to sell a million records. Because Jean was still legally underage, Ferlin became her guardian.

Jean later became a television favorite on the first country music network television show, "The Ozark Jubilee," which was broadcast coast-to-coast every Saturday evening on the ABC network.

On her 22nd birthday, November 21, 1955, Jean was invited to become a member of the Grand Ole Opry. Becoming an Opry member and working out of Nashville took Jean into many new parts of the country she'd never seen.

Also joining the Grand Ole Opry in1955 was a tall, handsome West Virginian named Hawkshaw Hawkins. Jean and Hawkshaw toured together and eventually married. They had a traveling Wild West show complete with horses and Indians. Hawkshaw was a tremendously talented individual, with "eleven-and-a-half yards of personality" to match. He was a well-loved man by fans and peers alike. Jean reveals in this book the Hawkshaw no one else knew. They had one son, and Jean was eight months pregnant with their second child when tragedy struck. Returning home to Nashville from a benefit concert for the family of a disc jockey in Kansas City, Hawkshaw died when the plane he was aboard crashed. This was the crash which took the lives of pilot Randy Hughes, and fellow Opry stars Cowboy Copas and Patsy Cline.

Hawkshaw did so much more for country music than just perish in a plane crash with Patsy Cline. He needs to be remembered for how he lived and what he contributed in his 41 years. In this story, Jean helps those who don't know about Hawkshaw understand that.

Ever the strong and courageous woman, Jean showed others around her and the country music fans just how much strength she had as a mother of one, losing a husband, and giving birth to a second son just one month later. Keep in mind this was many, many years before it became acceptable to seek greif counseling on how to survive during such life-changing events.

The Jean Shepard catalog of albums, singles, and hit records continued coming at a steady pace throughout the 1960s and '70s.

As the sound of country music started changing in the 1980s, Jean stood steadfast and committed to tradition. One night during this period on the "Grand Ole Opry," on mike after Jean's performance, host Bill Anderson asked innocently on the air, "Jean, what label are you recording for these days?" Jean fired back in a sharp and authoritative voice, "I'm not recording for any label right now, because there's no one in this town recording any country music."

Such comments are not unusual from Jean Shepard. She has always been known as someone who tells it like it is. The great thing about Jean is you always know where you stand.

Her music and personality are committed to what she believes is right. She is a Christian, strong-willed, and devoted to her music. In the more than 60 years she's been in the business, her talent, her voice, the songs she's sung, and her ability as an entertainer have never been in question.

Jean Shepard has legions of fans the world over. These are fans that she always has time for – whether it's a personal appearance or someone she might meet casually while out shopping somewhere.

On a personal note, thanks to my father I've known about Jean Shepard virtually my entire life. Back in the mid- to late 1950s, my father became an instant fan after seeing Jean in concert in Glen Echo, Maryland. That evening she was backed up by Lester Flatt & Earl Scruggs and their Foggy Mountain Boys, who were also on the show. After I reached my teenage years and began making some money, already a fan, I started buying Jean's records; and eventually I got to meet the singer I admired so very much. After beginning a career in broadcasting in Maryland, followed by more than a decade in Washington, DC, I played Jean Shepard's recordings on every program. Many times I would drive four and five hours each way to go see her in concert and became better acquainted. I served as the master of ceremonies for a number of her performances, and later she actually got me a job emceeing some shows as well. When the opportunity arose to come to Nashville and get a job with WSM and be considered for a position as a "Grand Ole Opry" announcer, Jean was a big supporter. As a fan and a friend, I can vouch that her kindnesses are things you just don't forget.

Jean Shepard is one who has never forgotten where she came from. For years, fans and friends alike have been diligent in requesting a book be written about her life's experiences. Among these experiences are a lot of great stories about fellow artists that will be new to just about every person who reads this book. Her journey thus far has been an amazing one, and thankfully for all of us who enjoy Jean and her music, the word retirement doesn't seem to be in her vocabulary. As this book goes to press, she recently celebrated her 80th birthday, her 58th anniversary as a continuous member of the Grand Ole Opry and her 45th wedding anniversary to Benny Birchfield.

There is much more to tell about Jean Shepard, but why not let Jean share the story in her own words. Let's begin reading, learning, and obtaining a deeper comprehension of a woman who has experienced and contributed so much.

One of her friends and fans,

—Eddie Stubbs, WSM Grand Ole Opry Announcer
Nashville, Tennessee

# DOWN THROUGH THE YEARS

Jean Shepard

Author: Shepard Jean

Down Through The Years / Jean Shepard

p. cm.

ISBN:978-0-944391-06-8

*Printed in the United States of America*

10 9 8 7 6 5 4 3 2 1 / 1 2 3 4 5 6 7 8 9 10

# TABLE OF CONTENTS

# CHAPTER ONE

# "WORK HARD AND BE TOUGH"

When my first song hit the charts I was so inexperienced that I didn't even know what a *Billboard* was. Ferlin Husky and I were traveling to Capitol Records' studio in Los Angeles after our record "A Dear John Letter" began to catch on. Our producer had heard from Slim Willet, a DJ in Texas, that it looked like "Dear John" could be a number-one song. Well I didn't really know what a number-one song was either. We were in two cars, there was several of us making this trip together, and the boys was talking about stopping for a *Billboard*; they was making bets where "Dear John" was on the charts. I remember thinking, Where in the world will we put a billboard? Strap it to the top of the car? Buck Owens bet it would be number two, Ferlin bet it was five, and Tommy Collins said three. We stopped, got a *Billboard*, read the charts, and Buck Owens said to me, "THAT'S a number-one record!" He pitched that *Billboard* to me (I was in the back seat), and he said, "You know what girl singer has a number-one record?"

I said no. Buck said, "You do, buddy."

There had been some who had told me, early on, there was no place in country music for a girl singer. I had said I was about to change that.

I was a California ranch hand's daughter barely a year out of high school, and I had the first million-selling song by a woman in country music since before WWII. Only weeks before "A Dear John Letter" started to soar, I was still singing and playing bass for an all girls' band.

———

The Melody Ranch Girls was a band my friends and I started when I was a high school sophomore. By my senior year we were playing every Friday night, Saturday night, and Sunday night. Weekend nights, my daddy was driving me to the dance halls around the San Joaquin Valley. Country music was big in California; plenty of great players and songs making the circuit of dance halls and community events. Daddy would strap my upright bass onto the top of the car, drive me to one of our shows, listen to us play until about one o'clock in the morning, pack up and drive me home, and then he'd get up at five a.m. to go to work. And he would enjoy every minute of it.

That shows you something about Daddy. He passed along his love of music, along with a lot of endurance. Even though I was young, I made a good start because of all my daddy and mother had passed on to me. I can't even tell you how they sacrificed to give me that chance. I wish everyone had a daddy and mother like mine. Do you know how I got my bass fiddle? They hocked every piece of furniture to scrape together three hundred and fifty dollars and buy one – because they knew I was going to play it, even though I had to teach myself, by ear. From our earliest years they had taught us to work hard and to be tough, and to have confidence.

I'd like to try to tell you what I can remember about my family. If you understand my early years, you'll understand where country music comes from.

California was not my first home. We moved out there from Oklahoma in 1943 or '44 to find work. I was born in Paul's Valley, Oklahoma, on November 21, 1933, to Hoit A. Shepard and Allie Mae Isaac Shepard. At that time I had an older brother and three older sisters. We lived on the banks of the Washita River. While we were building that home, we lost just about all our household goods to a fire. Then, the first year we lived in the house, we lost our corn crop to a flood. Everybody around us was poor. But it was sufficient – the Lord took care of it. We raised our own meat, and grew our own garden – it was the best in the world.

Materially our home was very poor, but we had all the love in the world. It was a very loving atmosphere. We were a family of twelve, and I was fifth. My greatest ally was my older sister LaQuita. Daddy was a farmer all his life, and he had the know-how for anything in this world that needs to be done. He had only a fifth grade education, but he was one of the wisest men I ever knew. Mother was a city girl, born and bred in the city, so she learned to be a farmer's wife the hard way. She learned by doing what had to be done and rising to the occasion. This was during the Dust Bowl, and at the beginnings of the Great Depression – that's what my parents were up against. But we loved one another, and we had a wonderful time. It was over too soon.

We lived within walking distance of my mother's parents. Her father, my Poppy Isaac, he was a Jewish man. A wonderful man – I can remember him coming in from work, and he would pick me up and throw me in the air. He was very loving. My grandmother was more cantankerous. She wanted things to be just so – if you have chores to do, get out and do it.

Mother made a beautiful garden, and she put up all our food, sewed our clothes from flour sacks – that's what she had, so that's what she used –

sewed them on a pedal sewing machine. In one way she set the pattern that I have lived by. My career, when I got started, would have a lot in common with hers; I came along at a time when the world of country music was stacked against me succeeding as a solo female singer. It would be a thing I learned the hard way, too. There would come only one time I ever felt like it was over, and when that time came, Mother was the one who wouldn't let me stay down.

---

Our home was sparsely furnished. It featured a wood cookstove, a wood-burning heater, a homemade table, two chairs, and benches for us kids to sit on. We had three sets of iron bedposts with coil springs. The cotton mattresses my mother and grandmother made was sprayed regularly for bedbugs. Mother made all the sheets, pillowcases, and quilts for our covers. We had an old library table where the older kids did their schoolwork. There was no electricity but we had three coal oil lamps.

The only entertainment that I can remember we had was an old RCA wind-up table model Victrola, commonly known now as a record player. No one those days had a Victrola, I can't think of anyone. Daddy valued music that much. It was my mother who could play piano and sing, and Daddy who was determined to save a penny here and a nickel there until he'd have enough to buy a record. We inherited music from our mother, and Daddy cultivated it.

There's a lot of musical talent in my brothers and sisters. You should hear my brother Hoit sing. He can sing better than any of the best country music legends ever thought about – Merle, Lefty, any of them. Then my brother Jerry – he is a very good drummer and had a band out in Montana for quite a few years. He played around Missoula and out in there. Home is where I learned to sing, right along with feeding chickens, tending cows, chopping weeds, and working hard to survive. I don't guess it seemed hard at the time; it was just how it was.

————

My first recall of my daddy was the job he had at the Paul's Valley Alfalfa Mill. He sewed the burlap sacks that they put feed in. He made approximately thirty-five cents a day. When I was about two years old, Daddy was asked to repair one of the grain elevators. He had to climb thirty to forty feet up to do the job. After he had completed the repair, he started down. Suddenly he lost his balance, fell, and broke his back. There was no insurance to take care of us, but some of the people at the mill would bring by food every so often. The older kids worked for other people picking cotton, or whatever, to help out. Mother even took in washing and ironing. Daddy was laid up for about six months.

My oldest brother was Billy Joe, and my oldest sister was Naomi; next came LaQuita, then Coy Lou, then me. Quita was left to babysit with me one day. I was about a year old and she was about six. It was a real hot summer, so all I had on was a diaper. She got to playing in the sand, building dirt houses, roads, and the like, and forgot all about the small one-year-old she was supposed to be watching. Being a curious child, and one who would get into anything, I decided to go for a hike along the river. After about an hour or so, Sis started to look for me and I was nowhere to be found. Sis tried to explain that I had been right there all the time, but she had been too busy playing and didn't really know where I was. Well they started looking. Daddy automatically started looking for my tracks, and found them heading toward the river. Of course, this brought on panic – my tracks led to the river and stopped!

Then Daddy remembered I always liked to go to my Mommy and Poppy Isaac's house. They were my mother's parents who lived in a dugout dwelling not far down the river.

Daddy headed down that way, and he met them coming our way; my grandpa had me by the hand and was on his way bringing me home. Needless to say, LaQuita's hide got tanned very properly.

————

Then there was the time when we were planting the garden. Having some black-eyed peas left over, I didn't know where to put them, or what to do with them. So I stuck one of them up my nose, not telling anyone what I had done. After about ten days or so, Mother noticed one side of my nose was swelling very badly. So looking up my nostril, she found a pea with about a two-inch sprout.

I remember waiting one day for the older kids to come home from school because I just had to tell them that I had been sick all day with a terrible earache. Mother had put some oil (what we called sweet oil, but commonly known as olive oil) in my ear to get rid of the ache. You know, even today, I cannot get out in the cold weather when the wind is blowing without having ear trouble.

————

We had a couple of milk cows and some baby calves then. We couldn't afford to feed them grain or hay, so the three older kids had to take real long butcher knives and cut what is known as johnson grass. It was put into bundles and carried to the stock. This one day, I remember Billy Joe, who was one very lazy boy, as most eleven- or twelve-year-old boys are, decided that Naomi and LaQuita was going to cut his share of the grass.

Quita, being like me, a very strong-willed kid, refused. Naomi was a little bit afraid of Bill. Well Quita and Naomi picked up their bundles of grass and started home.

Billy Joe got so mad, he picked up his knife and took out his anger with a big swing. Naomi was in back of the line, so the top of her head got laid open. She started bleeding very badly. When he saw the blood, he realized what he'd done. Quita rushed Naomi home, but Bill hid somewhere the rest of the day. Because we couldn't afford any kind of medicine or bandages, Mother had to depend on home remedies for everything. She knocked the stovepipe loose and covered the wound with soot. The soot that Mother took out of the stovepipe, thank goodness, made the blood clot, and she was able to get the bleeding to stop.

Well needless to say, Billy Joe didn't come home until he thought all of us were in bed asleep. We all were – except for one person, my daddy, who was waiting behind the door. When the door opened, Daddy grabbed him by the nape of his neck; and friends, he got the most deserved old-fashioned whipping a kid could ever get. As I said, he deserved it.

———

I was about three years old when Daddy decided that we would move from Paul's Valley to Hugo, Oklahoma. My other grandparents had moved there, my daddy's parents. We moved in with them for a while till we could build our house. Daddy made an agreement with Mr. and Mrs. Ethelbert Milburn to milk their cows and take care of their stock. By this time, Mother had had my younger brother Hoit, who we called Sonny; so there was six of us kids. We lived in a four-room house that was made out of round boxing planks, or unfinished lumber. During the summer, we like to roasted because it was so hot, and of course the winters were really, really cold. Our seventh sibling was born in this house, my brother Robert. He was our Valentine baby because he was born on February 14, and a lot of good memories go along with him. And he grew up to be the biggest character of all.

———

I remember once, all of us girls were outside playing – me, Naomi, Quita, and Coy Lou. We didn't have any screens on the windows so they were wide open. Now Quita happened to look in the window of Mother and Daddy's bedroom, and, oh, she started just laughing. She got us to come look. There stood my brother Bill in front of Mother's dressing mirror, flexing his skinny little muscles with nothing on but my mother's girdle. Of course us girls all got to laughing so hard, which brought on a lot of wrath from brother Bill. He picked up a piece of stove wood and threw it through the window at us. He was furious and hollered that he was going to kill us all. Bill, being a very ornery boy, was probably capable of it. All of us girls started yelling, "Run for your life." Well Bill came running out of the house with nothing but the girdle on, and carrying another stick of wood.

Quita, being a little smarter than the average bear, climbed into the tree that was out in the yard. Naomi started running down the trail towards Grandma and Grandpa Shepard's house, which was about a half a mile away. Quita kept yelling from her perch up in the tree, "Run, Naomi, run faster! Run for your life." Well Bill chased Naomi to the main highway before he realized that he didn't have anything on but the girdle. He came back and tried to get me and Coy Lou to tell him where Quita was. Of course we told him that we didn't know.

Grandma Shepard was a real heavy woman. She made us come

down to her house, to try to get to the bottom of what was going on. We told her the truth about it; but Billy Joe, of course, lied to her. He stayed across the road and wouldn't come to where she could get to him. She called to him, but he still wouldn't come over there. So she told him she was going to come after him. He told her she was too fat and couldn't catch him. Well she took a rock and proceeded to bean him with it. After she hit him with a couple of rocks, he decided he had better come over and sit on the porch with the rest of the kids.

———

From the Milburn farm, we moved to the Reed place, where Daddy had gotten a government loan. We farmed "on the halves" for Mr. Reed, which in layman's terms is what people call sharecropping. The government would give the sharecroppers money to plant their crop. The landowner got half of the profit; the government gave us the other half and took part of it out. That's sharecropping. He got his half, and – he got half of our half, too! My younger brother Jerry and sister Frances were both born while we lived at the Reed place.

Yes, we were sharecroppers. We raised cotton, sugarcane, peanuts – and needless to say, we were very, very poor. We didn't know it though, because we always had food and clothes, be what they may. Had it not been for raising a large garden, we probably would not have survived.

I remember my mother canning corn, peas, tomatoes, green beans, turnip greens, and cabbage to make kraut. We raised onions, potatoes, and sweet potatoes, which we buried under the house to get them through the winter so they wouldn't freeze and ruin. Mother canned our food in half-gallon jars the old-fashioned way, with a big heavy pressure cooker. She canned them in the half-gallon jars because quart jars were too small, as by this time there were eight of us kids.

We had an orchard that had pear trees, peach trees, apple trees, and wild plums. From this orchard, by the way, we made our jams, jellies, and canned fruit and stuff. Half of the stuff we picked we sold to the state prison at McAlester, Oklahoma. We also picked blackberries, but it was a real hard job because they grew wild.

I remember lots of times after picking blackberries all day, we'd go home and Mother would give us a bath, and scrub us with real harsh lye soap to try and kill chiggers. If anybody doesn't know what a chigger is, it is a very small red bug that attaches itself to your skin and just digs in. They're worse than mosquitoes, and they're just real hard to get rid of. Wild blackberries may be worth what you have to go through, because they taste better than any tame ones; but there was always the danger of snakes, hornets, and tarantula spiders. We never did get bit by any of them, so I guess the Lord was with us; or we were just lucky!

It was a hard, hard life. But we had a lot more than some had: which was nothing.

We didn't have the money to hire any help, so Mother and Daddy would go to our school and get a permit to keep us out of school until we got all of our crops in. We usually missed the first two months of school and really had to bust our butts to catch up. But you know, I never once remember any of us ever failing; we always made up our grades.

I told you Daddy only had a fifth grade education. That's the way it was for most farm families those days; he had to leave school because he was the oldest son of their family, and he had to help support them. The first school I ever remember going to was called Eggshell School. Daddy had gone there when he was a kid.

Around November and December of each year was hog-killing

time, when we usually killed four or five big hogs. We made our own bacon, ham, and sausage. Daddy also helped kill hogs for our neighbors. It was kind of a yearly ritual and the whole community took part in it. We even made sorghum molasses. This, too, was a community project because we ground sugarcane for all of our neighbors. They would bring their cane to us, and we would grind it up at the cane mill, and then Daddy made sorghum molasses for them.

We had to start cutting wood for the winter months ahead because we cooked and heated with wood. You know, I can never remember running out of wood. I do remember one time when I got hurt cutting up wood because of the dumb things kids can decide to do. Me and my sister Coy Lou were cutting wood. I was scrawny and the runt of the family, so I was sitting on a little log that was up on the wooden horses. She was sawing this pole, and she told me, "Put your leg up there and I'll saw it off for you." Well dumb me, I flopped my leg up there and, boy, she dragged that saw right down across my right kneecap. I still have the scars from it to this day. Of course, Mother whipped me and I don't know why, except Coy Lou said she figured that if I was that dumb, I needed a whipping.

A few weeks after the hog killing, it was soap-making time. Mother would take the hog's head, or feet, and whatever leftover fat there was and boil it in a big black kettle outside the house. (That was the same black kettle she would use to boil sheets in.) So she'd boil the hog's fat and add ashes and a can or two of lye; she'd stir and boil it for hours, and then let the fire go out at night. When she'd leave it overnight it would harden. Then it was cut into blocks and stored in the smokehouse along with the hams, sausages, and all the other meat.

We made something they called home brew. My family was never drinkers, but home brew I think was sort of like a strong beer. Mother would let it sit behind the cookstove one week and it would ferment. I don't know what it was made from; we grew grain, so it could have been that, or maybe something else? After that first fermenting period, she'd put it in quart jars. They'd bury it, to store it in the cool. One day we were eating Sunday dinner, sitting around the table all of us, eating fried chicken – and out behind the smokehouse we heard the awfullest bang. It was one of them jars! Exploded. It left a hole in the ground!

After working for six full days, Mother and Daddy made sure that we got to church on Sunday. Church was held in our schoolhouse; there was no church houses available as such. Sunday was always our day of rest, and usually all the neighbors and their kids would gather at our house for all kinds of games all afternoon. And my mother would play piano. I inherited my music from her. Daddy loved music, and Mother was the one who played; she sang a lot of harmony, too. Every Sunday, all of us who were there, we'd sing together.

We didn't have any school buses. The high school did, but not the elementary school. We walked two miles (one way) to school – that was four miles a day. We walked come hell or high water, rain, sleet, snow, or whatever. Many, many times I remember we walked in zero weather. When we got to school, the teachers would put our hands in cold water to keep them from getting frostbitten.

Now as a precaution from getting sick, we wore an herb called asafetida in these bags tied around our neck. Of course we kept them tucked under our clothes so the other kids wouldn't see them. But what was so funny, and what we didn't know, was that almost all the other kids had them on too.

We carried our lunches in what was called lard buckets (a little round half-gallon bucket with a wire handle on it). Our lunch usually consisted of what was left over from breakfast, maybe ham and biscuits, or sausage and biscuits, and maybe some sugar cookies left from the last baking day.

At the end of the school day, we never could stop to play, because we always had work when we got home. Each kid had certain chores that he or she had to do. Billy Joe was usually splitting wood, and brought it in for the stoves; and he also fed the hogs. Naomi helped Mother cook the evening meal. Quita was usually with Daddy, because she was more or less Daddy's right-hand "man" when it came to working in the fields. If she wasn't there, she was feeding the livestock or helping with the milking. Coy Lou gathered the eggs and fed the chickens; and me, I gathered the cows in from the pasture.

At this time we had about eleven cows. There was not such a thing as electricity at our house, so we did the milking by hand. Usually Quita, myself, and Daddy (when he was available) did the milking. I always had to get up at five a.m. to go get the cows. After we finished, we would turn them back out to the pasture because we didn't have hay to feed them.

All the chores we did in the morning was done before we went to school, and almost all of the chores had to be repeated every night after we got home. So that meant we had to do the same ones, over and over again.

All of us girls' school clothes were made out of flour sacks with matching underpants. Mother would go to the store and buy flour or sugar in fifty-pound bags. It would be a pretty flower or checkered pattern, something she could make a dress out of. She sewed all of our clothes on an old Singer pedal sewing machine. We only had two changes of clothes: two dresses, two underpants, and two petticoats that were made out of those flour sacks, which were like bleached muslin. We thought for years that Pillsbury was a clothing manufacturer because most of the time it was printed on the seat of our underdrawers, in big, bold letters – PILLSBURY.

We had one pair of shoes to last the whole school term. We had old, worn shoes to work in, of course, like old brogan boots. We always had to change our clothes the minute we got home from school, and put on our old work clothes, which usually consisted of a pair of bib overalls. We wore a lot of hand-me-down clothes given to us by various relatives. We wore long cotton stockings with garters made with a piece of elastic.

Very seldom back then did we see cars. I remember a gentleman who was a very precious old man, our postman, Mr. Oakes, had a car. I recall another time one morning when Coy Lou and I started walking to school. We had only gone about a quarter of a mile and a car came along. The driver stopped and was going to give us a ride. But Coy Lou, being the chicken that she is, was scared to death. Anyway, she wouldn't get in first, so she pushed me into the middle of the front seat. I found myself beside a very large man with one of the biggest pistols I had ever seen strapped to his waist. I was scared to death because I thought he was going to take us somewhere and shoot us. Little did either of us realize that we were very, very safe in the company of our sheriff!!

———

I remember our Christmases with a heart that is filled with love. They were wonderful and beautiful times. Mother would start baking a couple of weeks before, making all kinds of cakes, pies, puddings, homemade bread, and cookies. Daddy would take me and any of the other kids who wanted to go and find what we thought would be the right tree. Some of the other kids would gather holly berries. When we got ready, everyone would pitch in and help. But it would always be after the night's chores were done.

Mother would pop corn, which we used to string around the tree. We girls would take needle and thread and make long strings of popcorn mixed with the holly berries to wrap around the tree for decorations. We had a box of icicles that we must have used for ten years, using them over and over. We would take them back off the tree and reuse them again the next year. We also used some drawing paper, using red and green that we had brought home from school, and made some stars and little things like that to put on the tree.

The excitement of Christmas would build for two weeks. We never had stockings to hang as kids do nowadays. We never got any store-bought toys. We did get a few homemade toys. Each one of us had our own chair. We printed our name on a piece of paper and would stick it on the chair so Santa Claus would know which one was which. I remember one Christmas in particular when we older kids got a homemade wooden gun. It was called a zip gun. It had a finger hole, and on the back was a clothespin turned upside down, and with it there was three or four strips of rubber about ten inches long. You would stretch that rubber over the barrel of the gun, bring it back and clamp the two ends of it in the clothespin. When you press the clothespin open, the two pieces of rubber would burn a blister. Daddy made a rule that if any of us got caught shooting one another above the waist, he'd take the gun away and destroy it. You know, as I think back, when did my daddy carve those guns out of that rough wood? He was always working. I just wonder when did he get the time?

We couldn't wait for Christmas morning. When we got up out of bed and ran to look at our chairs, we usually found something like this: one orange, one apple, and sometimes a banana (if we were lucky). We would get maybe three or four walnuts, and some curly-Q candy that looked like candy cane (except that it was shaped like a bunch of S's tied together) and maybe three or four pieces of some other Christmas candy. What a treat; you'd think someone had given us the moon!

Christmas Day was the big feast. We ate all the goodies that Mother had worked (down to the bone) baking. Our excitement, I guess, lasted for another two weeks. Maybe one day we'd eat the apple, then the next day, we'd eat the orange. Then we'd stretch our Christmas candy as far as we could, on into the next two weeks.

As I look back now, we really lived in poverty. But we didn't know it; everyone around us lived the same way. My mother I don't think ever expected she was going to be blessed with ten children; but the winters were long and cold, you understand.

————

We had at this time the largest span of mules in Oklahoma. A span is the same thing as a team. Their names were Kit and John. I remember our daddy would hire himself and the mules out to work for other people for a big salary of fifty cents a day. My God, can you imagine that!

I remember Daddy having our horse, Bess, bred to a jackass so we could have another mule to use on the farm. Now a lot of people don't realize that you cannot breed a male and a female mule. To get a mule, you have to breed a jackass to a female horse. (Just thought I'd pass that little information on to you.) Well Bess rewarded us with several nice colts and we loved every one of them.

Every spring we'd get real excited because it was time to put up the martin birdhouses. The martin is a small purple-black bird, which eats flying insects and is popular around farms. Martins come to a certain kind of birdhouse; it has to be an open area. Daddy would make a large birdhouse with maybe twenty-five holes and compartments. Then he would put it way up on a twenty- to thirty-foot pole. It was always so much fun to watch these birds come in and settle into their houses.

We did all the farming with our mules and the mare. In the springtime we'd turn the ground with the big turning plow. A few weeks later, we'd mist the ground and turn the harrow over it and smooth it out. Then we'd take this big plow called a lister and we'd make the big furrows and plant the seeds. After that the only thing we could do was pray for rain and good weather to make them grow.

Around this time we bought another mule by the name of Alex. Daddy was told that the mule was mean, to be careful and not let us kids around him too much. We were taught to always watch the weather in Oklahoma, because at this time of year, the weather was pretty unstable. One time Coy Lou was plowing the lower cornfield with Alex. Well some pretty heavy, dark clouds came up and Coy Lou was thinking she didn't have much time before the storm would strike, so she decided to ride Alex home. It scared us real bad when we saw her coming up the lane on that darn mule. But we found out one thing – we could ride him. And I'll tell you another thing, the storm that moved in and dumped a couple of inches of rain wasn't nothing compared to the storm that Daddy rained down on Coy Lou's butt.

One thing we all learned when we were young, that when Mother and Daddy set up rules and told us what to do or what not to do, they meant every word they said. If we didn't live by the rules, there was not time for twenty questions and answers. The answers came from Daddy's double razor strap.

Now some of you might think that my daddy was a very stern and harsh man. But let me assure you one thing, he was not. He was without a doubt the most loving and gentle man that God could ever put on this earth. I only wish that everybody in this world could have had a daddy like mine.

He was fun-loving; he loved pulling a prank. He might send the younger kids to go out and play in Mother's flowers – Mother could grow anything, and she worked to get the flowers looking just like she wanted them; so she'd get mad if anybody messed it up. Daddy would just die laughing; she knew he was pulling her leg. Mother kept her house so orderly and clean; she made up the beds pretty with chenille bedspreads, and you could drop a quarter on it and it'd bounce. So Daddy might send us to go in and play on the bed – just to see her jump us, "Get offa my beds!"

It's like this. He gave us love in every possible way. When I was about three he ran into a burning tent to pull me out of the fire. He had been up there waterproofing this tarp where all our household belongings was stored while we built our house. I was under the tent by the kerosene stove to keep warm. Some of his paraffin dropped down from the roof to that stove, bust into flames, and the fire got me right on my right arm (there's still a scar). Daddy run in there into the flames, snatched me out, caught fire; my grandfather had to jump him and roll him in the sand to put him out. We both had to be taken to the hospital. His left arm was burned through to the bone. He saved my life.

He was the most loving man in the world. We felt it every day. So even his discipline showed he loved us. He expected us to live by what we know is right. He knew we had to learn that, so we'd have what it takes to live in this world.

So if my daddy told us to do something and we didn't do it, the second time he told us he would call us by our full name. He might say, "Ima, it's time to feed the chickens." It'd be about five o'clock at night. Well if I didn't get up and go right then, he would say, "Ollie Imogene, go do what I tell you." I knew that when he called me by my full name, I had better get up off my can and do what he said or it would be the double razor strap. That was a way of life.

Daddy was the kind of man – you weren't going to very often hear the words, "I love you," but he would lay his hand on your shoulder when he walked by; you could just feel the love. You felt it when you was with him, and you felt it by the things he would do for you. He did everything in his power to keep us safe and happy, and knowing right from wrong is one of them. But there was a lot of trials to go through; right and wrong is hard to learn.

———————

One time while we lived in Hugo, my mother had to go to Paul's Valley because my Poppy Isaac had had a heart attack. (He lingered on for several months before he died.) Mother rode the bus to Paul's Valley and Daddy stayed home, but was out working all day. There was this Mr. Ellington who lived about a mile from us. He told Mother and Daddy that he would watch us kids. Billy Joe was about sixteen, Naomi was a couple years behind him, Quita was about twelve, and Coy Lou was next in line. I was about seven or eight years old.

This Mr. Ellington had a daughter named Opal. She was down at the house when Billy Joe started trying to bully Quita around. Naomi was always kind of afraid of Billy Joe, her and Coy Lou – he would intimidate them. He wasn't big enough to intimidate me, even if he was six feet tall when I was three feet tall; I wouldn't let him! That really went against the grain with him. Quita was the same. She always stood up to Billy Joe. Well he was trying to make her cut the wood, or whatever, and make her do all his chores. She said she wasn't going to do them. He started banging her around, slapping her. Seems like he had her pushed up against the wall, and Daddy's .22 was up over the door. So she reached up over the door and got Daddy's .22 rifle; she said she was going to kill him.

Well she shot it! Billy Joe slumped over – we all thought he was dead! It scared me to death. Quita said, "Go get Mr. Ellington." Like I said, Opal Ellington was there and saw everything.

I run ahead because I could run like a deer – real fast. I had run about three quarters of a mile, and I met Mr. Ellington coming towards our house. He knew something was wrong.

I said, "Quita shot Billy Joe."

Mr. Ellington, who was about sixty years old, started running with me back to the house. When we got there, we saw that Billy Joe had come to. What it done was, it scared him so bad that he fainted.

We didn't want to tell Mother and Daddy. We knew Daddy would tan Billy Joe's hide. I think the kids patched the bullet hole where you couldn't see it. But my daddy had a sixth sense. When he got in that evening, he hadn't been in the house an hour when he looked around that room and he knew that gun had been moved. He had always said to keep away from them guns. He had a shotgun and a .22. Well he looked at all of us and said, "Who's been messing with my gun?"

There was complete silence. You know, we didn't want to tell him nothing. But we finally told him what had happened. It's a wonder that bullet didn't hit Billy Joe.

————

Billy Joe was downright mean until he was about twenty-five or thirty years old. I don't know why he was so rebellious and mean. Billy Joe just was ornery. Even when he got grown, for a while he used to do things – he embarrassed me a couple times at my shows, just out there being a loudmouth. I'd tell the audience, "He puts me in mind of a catfish: all mouth, no brains." I ignored him finally; I ignored him for probably thirty years. Maybe I'm a bad person, but I can only put up with so much of that stuff; and pretty soon, when it gets up to the top of my head, I'm ready to chuck it off and say, Hey, go for it, do whatever you want to do.

But in later years he was a good person. I'll tell you when we finally patched things up. He was in the hospital, with serious heart trouble; and one of his girls called me and told me. My mother said to me, "Honey, you need to call Billy Joe and make peace with him." And I did. We would visit each other after that. He lived about ten more years.

———

Now my mother, as you have seen, was a wonderful woman. But she had this shortcoming: she played favorites. She coddled Billy Joe a lot, and coddled Naomi, my oldest sister. Then with Quita she kind of skipped over. Then with Coy Lou she coddled, and then she skipped over me. They were kind of her favorites, you know. They just got away with more than Quita and me. Maybe that's why the two of us was always allies; we would just stand back-to-back to fight the world if we had to.

All of my brothers and sisters are good people. They really are. But Mother did have favorites. She would make excuses for Billy Joe and for Naomi; and Coy Lou would just kind of whine around Mother and get her way. Coy Lou was a good person. We just recently lost her and it broke my heart, because we all try to stay very close. Naomi, too, we lost right as we were finishing up this book. Naomi was a very loving sister and good person. She always tried to keep the family intact, even though she was in California and I was in Nashville and Jerry's in Montana; we've got Frances in Arkansas and Carolyn and Sonny (Hoit) in California; then Quita lived in Lebanon, Tennessee, until we lost her in 2011. We've lost Robert, Quita,

Coy Lou, Bill, and now Naomi too.

Daddy wouldn't let Mother work in the fields. But let me tell you, our mother probably worked harder than any of us. Even if she had wanted to work out in the fields, she was busy taking care of the household chores like cooking, canning, changing diapers, washing and ironing, and whatever had to be done.

As I told you, one of my chores was to bring in the cows every morning and night. Well it got to be a tiresome job. Daddy had bought a young Jersey bull and we named him Oscar. Daddy wouldn't let me ride any of the mules or Bess to bring the cows in because they were used to plow with. But I decided that I needed some kind of transportation. So guess what? Oscar the bull was elected.

Now keep in mind, no one knew what I was up to. I rode him around the cow lot for several days with no witnesses. By this time, Oscar was getting to be a good size bull. He probably weighed between six and eight hundred pounds. Also he wasn't the friendliest bull in the world. He could get pretty mean if he wanted to.

Oscar would run in the pasture with the cows, so when I'd go get them, I'd just hop up on Oscar's back. Here we'd come, bringing the cows home. This went on for several months without anybody ever really knowing what was going on. I was doing real good until one day when Mother and Daddy had gone to town in the wagon to buy our monthly supplies, such as flour, sugar, and the like. I was riding Oscar up the lane bringing the cows home. But little did I know that this would be my last bull ride.

The two brothers younger than me, Sonny and Robert, were hunkered down behind a big pole that the electric company had put into the corner of the cow lot to carry the new electric wire through the community. As I rode past them on Oscar, they jumped out and hollered and screamed at the top of their lungs. Well Oscar threw me and started pawing the ground. I knew he was going to get real mean; so, even though there was no opening under the fence, I went under the fence. I made an opening! Who knows – had I continued with this, I may have become the first female rodeo bull rider in the world!!

———

I was about eight or nine years old by this time. I remember one summer we needed extra money, so Daddy took me, Quita, Coy Lou, and Sonny to Frederick, Oklahoma. We spent the summer picking cotton for different farmers around the area.

We stayed in this old house and slept on our cotton sacks, and cooked over an open fire outside. I recall one night after we had eaten supper, we were sitting in the house talking about how much cotton we had picked, and how much money we had made. Daddy would get paid at the end of every day. We made approximately fifty cents per hundred pounds. Well while we were talking about our earnings, all of a sudden, we heard a noise. Because of the bad weather, the windows and doors were wide open. When we looked up, we saw listening at our back door one of the biggest black men I had ever seen in my life. He was probably at least six and a half feet tall and must have weighed two hundred twenty-five pounds.

My daddy asked him, "What the hell do you want?"

He said, "I don't want anything."

Then my daddy said, "You had better get the hell out of here."

The man left, and we never saw him again. Needless to say, we were scared to death, and it took a long time for us to go to sleep that night. I think my daddy stayed awake most of the night because he thought we might be robbed – we needed the money so desperately to make our government loan payment.

# CHAPTER TWO

# I'M GOING TO CALIFORNIA

About this time Mother and Daddy had bought a battery radio through the Montgomery Ward catalog. I'm telling you it cost a fortune. Daddy scrimped and saved because he wanted that radio so bad. I think it cost $12.98 plus $2.80 for the battery. It was real heavy, weighing about twenty-five or thirty pounds. Daddy set it on the library table in the living room. We couldn't listen to it much because we was afraid it would wear the battery down. Mother, while she was doing her work, would listen to three radio soap operas. I think their names were *Stella Dallas*, *Ma Perkins*, and *Pepper Young's Family*. They were each fifteen minutes long. When we would come to eat our noonday meal, we got to listen to the Light Crust Doughboys doing a live show from Tulsa, Oklahoma. The leader of this group was a gentleman by the name of Bob Wills. Their theme song went something like this: "Now listen everybody from near and far, if you wanna know who we are, we're the Light Crust Doughboys from the Burris Mills."

I think it was at this time that I became aware of the music that later would become my life and my livelihood.

Bob Wills became the highlight of my workday. And what became the highlight of our week was the *Opry*. Any other time except when these shows was on, they wouldn't let us turn on that radio. Didn't want to use up the battery.

On Saturday night after all the work was done, we couldn't wait – because we knew about eight o'clock, it was time for the *Grand Ole Opry* to come on. Daddy would get us all in the living room and we'd all have to sit perfectly still. We couldn't make a sound! Daddy had to hear every word of it.

We loved Roy Acuff, the Possum Hunters, Sam and Kirk McGee, Uncle Dave Macon, and the Gully Jumpers. A very dear man, whom I learned to love later on, was a man by the name of Cousin Lew Childre. With his dobro guitar, he would sing his favorite song, "I'm Alabama Bound." Daddy thought he was the greatest. But for some silly reason or another we kids didn't like him.

Also at that time Daddy was buying a lot of Jimmie Rodgers records, Bob Wills, Riley Puckett, Gid Tanner and the Skillet Lickers, Blind Boy Fuller, and an occasional Roy Acuff record. Now keep in mind, Daddy would save a penny here and a penny there until he scrimped up enough to buy a record. I think the records cost ten or twelve cents, but it would take sometimes six or eight months to save up ten or twelve cents. All these years later, Daddy's record collection managed to remain in the family; my brother Jerry in Montana still has them.

I didn't realize that my future was being influenced by all of these great entertainers. I remember I was trying to learn all of their songs, and trying to yodel like Jimmie Rodgers. Of course all of the kids would get mad and want me to shut up. I'd be out on the porch swing or standing on Mother's wash bench singing at the top of my lungs. They told me it sounded like cattle bawling.

Mother had three big washtubs she did laundry in. She'd boil sheets in the iron kettle, and wash them in one tub with lye soap, and put them in the next one with bluing (and get the sheets so white they'd blind you). I remember I used to get up on Mother's washtubs and I'd just sing. I might sing a Jimmie Rodgers song:

I'm going to California,
Where they sleep out every night;
I'm leaving you baby,
'Cause you know you don't treat me right....

By looking at many country music performers, you'd see similar beginnings. You can see now what we weren't aware of at the time: that as farmers kept migrating west, California was receiving all this music. Over the '40s and '50s those of us who loved country music were mixing; you'd see the outcome of it all by the time my career took off. Then the whole nation was listening to our songs. Buck Owens, and so many people who made country music great and kept it country – where they came from is a lot like my story.

Millions had been migrating out of farm states like Oklahoma in those years; agriculture had not recovered from the Dust Bowl and Depression. It was impossible to make a decent living. California was a good place to get work, and some friends of Mother and Daddy had been there; they had kept in touch. Daddy decided to make the move to California around August of 1944. I was almost eleven years old.

To pay our way, we had an auction and sold all the furniture and livestock that we owned. One of the few times that I saw my mother cry was the day we sold her Singer pedal sewing machine. She had used that machine to make all of our clothes. I felt that she was seeing a way of life being left behind. She broke down and cried like a baby.

My daddy went out ahead of us to find work, he and Quita. Mother and the rest of us came out six or eight months after that. We rode a troop train; it was full of American GIs. It took about three days to get to California, and we stood ninety percent of the time. Mother was pregnant with my baby sister Carolyn, who is now sixty-eight. Finally one of those GIs getting on noticed my mother standing up, and he said, "Ma'am, take my seat." So we finally sat down. That made such an impression on me, I would never forget that young soldier.

The house we moved into at first had no electricity, so Daddy dug an open pit in the backyard. Mother cooked over that pit for about a month. We made pallets and slept on our cotton sacks. After a few months, we were able to buy some used furniture. Our life was still uphill going, but we were making a better living. I tasted beef for the first time in my life. Before, it was only pork and chicken – what we could raise.

In California our life got a little easier. We worked on a ranch; we worked for a Mr. Royben I think was the name, a nice man, for several years.

Dad was a ranch hand, and all our family worked with him – except, not Mother; we'd pick cotton and we'd cut grapes and lay them out in the sun to turn into raisins. Mr. Royben had a peach orchard and we would pick peaches. There were crews of workers, and I got tied in with a group of guys picking peaches. Dad told us to get six or eight lugs of peaches a day. (A lug is probably about a half a bushel.) I would sing a song every once in a while. The crew got where they'd request songs. So I'd say, I'll sing for half a lug of peaches. Then I'd sit up on top of my ladder and I'd sing. I always made my quota.

My mama got wind of it and she said, "You don't need to be entertaining those boys."

I said, "I want to entertain. I want to keep singing as much as I can."

So somebody would say, Jean sing this song – sing Jimmie Rodgers – or whatever; and I'd cut loose. I'd sit up at the top of my ladder; boy I'd rear back and let go.

I was about twelve years old, and that was my first experience in giving people what they wanted. If I didn't know the song I'd go home and learn it.

So I've been performing now for about seventy years. I am sure I know the words to five hundred songs by heart. We had a Grand Ladies show over in Branson about ten or fifteen years ago, and when we had request time, they never could stump me. Every request they didn't know the words to, they started saying, "Ask Jean. Jean knows it!"

———

I was supposed to start the third grade when we moved to California. The teacher asked me if I could handle fourth grade level. I said I didn't know, but I would try. It was hard at first, but then I just fell right in and did real good work. So I actually skipped third grade and went right to the fourth grade. And that was why I was seventeen at the time I graduated from high school.

I graduated from the eighth grade at Lynnwood Elementary School and started Visalia Union High School in September of 1947. There were a bunch of guys and girls there who loved to play country music. As a matter of fact, country music was an accredited course at Visalia High School! Visalia is about eighty miles north of Bakersfield. This was an area rich in just what it took to start a lot of careers that would go on to influence country music for decades – the rest of the century. We was just playing the music we knew. Not until "A Dear John Letter" got national fame did the music industry believe in the California country music.

————

At Visalia High I was in the Glee Club and also took some music courses. The school wanted my friends and me to play some music for this special show. The high school band director, Mr. Cline, admitted that he really didn't know much about country music, but we should be given the chance to play. He said he would oversee the performance.

Those of us who played and sang country music were not necessarily accepted by all the kids. A lot of Californians used the term "Okie" as an insult. What they thought of us, they thought of our music, too – thought they were above it I guess. So some kids at school would make fun of us. They would snicker and made snide remarks all the time. At the same time, those kids from town were always eager to trade lunches with us! We never had store-bought bread (everybody from the country called it light bread). They'd always bring maybe a peanut butter or bologna sandwich, or something like that, and I'd have a biscuit and sausage. They thought that was great.

But twenty-five years later, when my high school had a Jean Shepard Day in my honor, a lot of those grown-up kids came out and paid to see me play.

One of the students who snickered at me for singing country music was a girl named Glena Manker, who was the belle of the school. Anyway she was dating some boy from a motorcycle club, which, by the way, was a pretty good bunch of kids. This cute guy named Paul gave me his school sweater. Well Glena saw me wearing his sweater and got real jealous. A couple of years after I joined the Grand Ole Opry, I got a letter from Glena. She asked if I would please sign a picture and send it to her because there were some people that wouldn't believe that she knew me. Needless to say I didn't send her one.

––––––––

As I said, in high school, I majored in Glee Club and music. One day I was pulled out of my music class by the Glee Club director. They were going to do an assembly program that the whole school was going to attend. The boys' Glee Club was doing "Tumbling Tumbleweeds" as one of their songs, and they wanted me to yodel behind their singing. So he asked me to come, and I just couldn't do it; you know, I was fourteen or fifteen years old, and there in front of all your peers? I was afraid I would mess up. I said no.

But it was somewhere around that time that the all-girl band I've told you about would have its beginnings. I was a sophomore when me and some other girls I met decided we wanted to play country music together. We had this girl who played steel guitar by the name of Bonnie Cantrell. Jerri Starling played piano, and her sister, Wenell Starling, played lead guitar. We had a drummer, Shirley Vineyard. A girl named Frances played accordion. Then someone had to play bass. Guess who was elected? I had no idea how to play, but Mother and Daddy, as I told you, hocked all of our furniture to buy me an upright bass. I would sit and play on that bass to find the right frets. I learned to play it by myself, with a little help from the other girls.

Later we added Mary Pillow; she was a good fiddler. And Dixie Gardner played piano.

We started playing for dances and picnics in the community and we got pretty professional. At that time, drinking age was twenty-one in California. We were all underage. But the dance halls had what they called a beer garden. We worked the dance halls even though we couldn't go to the beer garden. It was all separate. So many of those places – the Pine Burr

Dance Hall, Happy Go Lucky, the Tagus Ranch – they all had beer gardens. Of course my mother and daddy, they just went in to listen to the music. It was a different world than I was brought up in.

I remember we would get paid five bucks and we would give it to our local deputy sheriff, a wonderful man by the name of Sandy Robinson. Sandy would usually give it back to us. He later became the sheriff of Visalia. He has since passed away, but he was good to us.

We met this man, Noble Fosberg, who decided more or less to manage us. We became known as the Melody Ranch Girls because around Hanford, California, he had a place called Noble's Melody Ranch. It was when I was with the Melody Ranch Girls that I met Hank Thompson.

I heard such great music there, there's nothing like it. I remember he had a man named Smiley Maxedon there, Noble did; he was a *good* singer – and never did get a break. That's one of many voices nobody now will get to hear, because you can't find any records by him; maybe one or two 45s. I'd go see him every chance I got. He would sing T. Texas Tyler's "Deck of Cards" and songs like that. A good singer.

Noble's Melody Ranch was one of a handful of dance halls in the area that attracted performers like Ferlin Husky, Hank Thompson, Johnny Horton, Johnnie & Jack and Kitty Wells, Lefty Frizzell, the Maddox Brothers & Rose. There was kind of a circuit. There was two local places Hank could sing: the Happy Go Lucky and the Melody Ranch – I think there was a place in Fresno also. So I would go hear him. Whenever Hank would come through I would get up onstage and sing with him. Hank would sing "The Wild Side of Life" and I'd sing the answer, "It Wasn't God Who Made Honky Tonk Angels."

When the time was right, the contacts made with Hank and these others would give me the big launch that led to a lifetime career. Hank told his producer at Capitol, Ken Nelson, "I've found this little girl who can sing; I think she's going to be big."

At the time Ken didn't want to give me a contract. He said, "There's no place in country music for women. But every band needs a girl singer."

By the time Noble became our manager, most of the girls had graduated. But remember, I was still in high school. In addition to Noble's, which was always our home base, we were working Fridays, Saturdays, and Sundays. On Fridays we would work in Paso Robles. On Saturdays we would work in San Luis Obispo, and on Sunday nights we worked in Oceano. Oceano was about a hundred-and-fifty-mile mountainous drive, and you understand this was before super highways.

So that was quite a drive every Monday in the wee hours. It took three, four hours to drive. We would play the dance on Sunday, ride all night, and get home just in time for me to catch the school bus.

I had a couple of teachers that were lenient and let me sleep in class. Mr. Curtis, my history teacher, was very lenient with me. He gave me a B in the class when I would have gotten a C or D. My Glee Club teacher was very lenient too. I don't know how I managed that last year in high school. The load was really very heavy and I was always so tired.

During the time I worked with the all-girl Melody Ranch Girls, I did ninety percent of the singing. After a while it caused me to have a husky, deep voice.

The memories I have of working with those girls are something else. Friends, have you ever seen eight women fighting? I never did really fight with them, but I argued and fussed with them. The piano player was a little older than some of us and started dating the drummer's father. The drummer didn't like this at all. One night as we left the stage after the show was finished in Oceano, California, all hell broke loose. The piano player and drummer were fighting like two wildcats. I started to feel like I'd had enough of that.

The place where we played on Saturdays was at a military base called Camp San Luis Obispo. I'll never forget one of the soldiers we always used to play music for; this was the time of the Korean War. They were a good bunch of guys to play for; we really got to know them. Vernon Lipp, this one boy, he rode a motorcycle. He used to help us when we were loading up; he was like family. One night he left and we didn't see him again for months. No one knew how to get in touch with him. Well he finally did show back up, and it turns out he'd had a wreck that night after he left. It literally scalped him. We all started crying. It had taken him all those months to heal.

———

One of the girls, Dixie Gardner, was married. Her husband's brother came home from the Navy and brought this friend with him named Freddie. Freddie had graduated from high school and joined the Navy. He started hanging around the dance jobs talking with me. I wasn't serious but he was. Next thing I knew, he asked me to marry him. All the other girls were getting married, and I thought he was a very nice guy, so I said yes. But when he brought me the ring, I was having second thoughts.

I told him, "No, I'm not ready to get married."

He didn't like that at all. He even threatened to kill me if I didn't marry him. I found out later that he had a medical discharge from the Navy; he had problems. But I didn't know it at the time. I told him not to threaten me or I would tell my daddy. Even though I was scared, I ended up marrying this man after I turned eighteen. It was either late in 1951 or early 1952. The marriage was only to last six months.

At first, my attitude was that I was going to try and be happy. But he became scarier after we married. I caught him in some lies. And he would make threats that really scared me to death. One day he told me he would kill my daddy. But he didn't physically abuse me at that time.

We had a little apartment in a house with front steps. We would sit out there quite a bit. This one night we were sitting out front, and the neighbor boy next door was fooling around and squirted me with a water pistol. So I picked up this glass of water and threw it at him. Freddie became so angry, I ran into our bathroom and locked the door. I told him I wasn't coming out until he cooled down. Well he hit the door and broke it down. But I think when he hit the door and it opened, it must have jarred his senses back.

Ironically, Freddie was from Tennessee. When I'd met Hank and he had asked me if I wanted a contract, Freddie tried to figure out some way to prevent it. He did not want me to record. It would have been extra money, and maybe that's part of it; I was making a hundred and twenty a week (sixty per show), and I could start making more than he was – that may have been part of the problem. Anyway he started to try and lay a plan to get me to go to Tennessee. He told me he had two brothers back home and that one of them had died. We didn't have any money, so I asked Noble for money for one plane ticket. It was for him to go see his mother and family. Well he didn't like it when I said I couldn't go. He wasn't having none of it. So he didn't go.

About three weeks later, I got a call from his mother – she just kinda chatted and caught up, and didn't say a word about her son dying. After that, maybe two weeks later, I was cleaning out a jacket of Freddie's to take to the cleaners. In the pocket was a letter from his mother. I saw where she'd written, "Me and the boys are fine," and I knew his brother had not died at all. I totally believed that he would have taken me to Tennessee and kept me there, barefoot and pregnant.

That's when I told my family all the things that had been happening.

So I moved back home with Mother and Daddy, and Billy Joe and my daddy knew about the threats and so forth now. So when Freddie came looking for me, my daddy – so even tempered – Daddy told him to get out and don't ever come back.

My mother went to court with me and talked to the judge. When I told him all I knew, he granted me an annulment.

Sometime in the next few weeks Freddie asked my sister Naomi's husband for a hundred dollars for my rings (Naomi had said she wanted them). I didn't know about it, and my sister thought I did. She came over one day and said, "I want your rings." He sold those rings right off my hand.

————

But I would rather think about the wonderful things that were happening at that time. That was a sour note, but I never let it keep me down. Let me tell you the story of how I came to meet one of my first music heroes, Bob Wills.

As a child in Oklahoma, working the fields every day, there was a time when I got through the day by waiting to hear Bob Wills. Mother liked to listen to her noon radio show, and Bob Wills was the young man who played fiddle for the band that sang the theme song. I loved hearing it. Mother made sure she called me in so I could listen. I could endure all morning looking forward to that.

Later Bob formed his group the Texas Playboys. When they come through California, of course, we had migrated there. So every time Bob would come out, I would go see him. One of my dreams was to be able to sing with Bob Wills one day.

Well sure enough, after I got into music, I had a chance one night to sing with Bob Wills. I want to tell you right here and now, friends, I was singing with him and he stepped up there beside me and did one of his little "Ah - ha's" – it thrilled me so much I thought I was going to have a convulsion. Now this is the truth. It was such a thrill, and I could not believe it.

I became pretty good friends with Bob. But before that, I remember one time he came to Bakersfield, to the ballroom Rainbow Gardens. His guys was setting up the equipment and I was sitting there talking to him. He knew that I had aspirations of being a singer, you know, and he just had a new record coming out.

I said, "Bob, why don't you go by the radio station and plug your new record?"

He said, "Sweetheart, you see that old man sitting over there?" There was an old man sitting across from us.

I said, "Yes, I do."

"That's my daddy.  He told all of us boys, 'So you want be in the music business, you want to make records? Okay. But I'll tell you one damn thing, if I ever catch any of you boys going by a radio station and asking a disc jockey to play your records, I'll kick your ass up between your shoulders'."

He said, "And the old man can still do it."

I thought, Wow. But his daddy still had a lot of influence on him. He had several brothers; there was Luke Wills, who was – well he and Bob both drank quite a bit. Then there was Billy Jack, who had a big dance hall called Wills Point in Sacramento, and Johnny Lee, who had a rodeo in Tulsa, Oklahoma, for many years. I loved every one of them. They were really into their music.

I loved the man who sang with Bob Wills, a gentleman by the name of Tommy Duncan.  I cannot say enough about Tommy Duncan.  He was the greatest western swing singer that has ever been.  I am just putting Tommy in along with Bob Wills. His great voice was just as important to the Texas Playboys as Bob himself was.

So I went to see them one time at the old Happy Go Lucky Ballroom in Tulare, California. I always got there about an hour before time because I wanted to talk with everybody. Tommy came over to me and said, "Well sweetheart, the next time you see the Texas Playboys, I won't be with them."

It crushed me; it broke my heart. I said, "Oh, you are kidding me?"

He said, "No."

Well everybody knew that Bob drank quite a bit.

Tommy said, "Let me tell you something, if I'm gonna run a band, it's gonna be my own. I've run this one for the last ten to twelve years."

I didn't see him for about a year or so, when he came through and played at the same place. I went to see him, and it was Tommy Duncan and the All-Stars. I will never forget that.

About ten years later, when the old Disc Jockey Convention used to be held at the Andrew Jackson Hotel here in Nashville, I walked through the door one day, and there stood Tommy. He was kind of leaning up against the wall. I walked by him and didn't realize that it was him. I turned around and went back and I said, "Oh my God, it's so good to see you."

He said, "I was just wondering if you was gonna walk by me and not speak to me."

I looked around at all these people who were passing him and I thought, Don't you people know who this man is – what he has meant to the western swing music industry? He is the greatest in the world! And so many of them didn't know who he was. That was heartbreaking. Of course, I loved him and wanted the whole world to know him. I loved Tommy Duncan and I loved Bob Wills.

I'll tell you about the last time I saw Bob. It was in the early '70s. It was when we played San Antonio, Texas. He was in the hospital. We played the show with Merle Haggard, Bill Carlisle, and the Osborne Brothers. Haggard wasn't feeling any pain that day, let me tell you. There was two phone booths near the back door. I was just coming out of one of the booths, from calling home to see if everything was okay. The back doors opened and in come Bob Wills with two Texas highway patrolmen. I stepped out of the phone booth, and I said, "Oh, Bob, what are you doing here? You are supposed to be in the hospital!"

Bob was really pale and looked bad. He put his arm around me and said, "Oh, sweetheart, I couldn't let my friends come to my town and not be here to meet them and be with them."

I put my arm through his and we walked over to the stage. The people were really rough on Haggard because it was plain that he was just in no shape to really be there.

I kept going, "Psst, psst!" to get Merle's attention, which took about two minutes. But I finally got his attention. He looked over and saw Bob. Instant sobriety come over Merle Haggard – because he loved Bob Wills. Bob went out and said a few words, and that was the last time I saw Bob.

# CHAPTER THREE

# NO PLACE FOR A WOMAN

I got up and sang a song with Hank Thompson one night, and he asked me if I'd like a recording contract.

I said, "Yes sir, I sure would."

He said, "I'll see that you get one."

I had high hopes. But as I kept working and waiting, the weeks added up. It would be several months before I heard anything from Capitol. In the meantime, I was busy singing every chance I could and enjoying all the wonderful entertainers we got to know. One of the singers who used to come play at Noble's Melody Ranch was Johnny Horton. He was just one of the nicest persons you would ever want to meet. I loved hearing him sing. You remember his ballad, "The Battle of New Orleans." He was living in Louisiana and was often on *Louisiana Hayride*, but came out to California several times and worked with us.

Johnny was probably one of my first boyfriends. It wasn't a big love affair, it was just two people who enjoyed being around one another. When we were in Oceano, we walked and talked on the beach, picked up seashells. It was a very innocent relationship. Years later he married

Billie Jean, who had been married to Hank Williams. When I went to play on *Louisiana Hayride*, Johnny met me as I was coming in and he said, "Don't say anything about our love affair. Billie Jean is very jealous." I said (laughing), "What love affair?" It was just a beautiful friendship.

Well Johnny Horton wanted to see me make a career; he had a lot of faith in my talent. It was Johnny's idea that I ought to make what we call a dub recording, something like a demo tape; it was a little acetate record. So I did a little session with him. He played guitar and we recorded "It Wasn't God Who Made Honky Tonk Angels." This was the record that Hank took to Ken Nelson at Capitol so he could hear my singing.

About the same time I had signed a recording contract with Mercury Records, but this was short-lived. They said for me to see Mr. D Kilpatrick, who was with Mercury. Well they called and said they had used up their entire budget for that year, so I didn't get to record. The contract wasn't any good anyway because I was underage, so we tore up the contract.

When Hank Thompson came back to California about four or five months later and asked me if I had heard from Capitol Records, he was embarrassed when I said I hadn't heard anything.

He said to me, "You shall."

About a week later I had a contract. I was nineteen years old.

They didn't believe in girl singers very much back then. I told you what Ken had said: "There is no place in country music for women singers." And he said, "But every band needs a girl singer."

I'd heard that before: once I was introduced to Hank Williams Sr. in 1952 at the Happy Go Lucky dance hall. He told me, "There ain't many women in country music." I told him that I was about to change that. He said, "Good luck to you, sweetheart."

I'm proud I got to meet the great Hank Williams. It was only a few months to a year before his tragic death. Speaking of Hank Williams, that reminds me of my first meeting backstage with Lefty Frizzell.

————

Lefty Frizzell is my favorite and probably the greatest male country singer that has ever been. He had a way with a song that no one could imitate; and many did try. Many of the great singers learned from listening to him.

The first time I met him was in California. I was just getting started as a singer with the all-girl band. He came to Visalia to sing when I was going to school and singing around in that part of the country. Hank Williams had just died, and Lefty got on the stage that night and said, "I want to do a song in memory of my good friend Hank Williams."

Everybody knew that Lefty had a bad drinking problem. On this occasion he was feeling no pain. He was going to sing "Kaw-liga." So he started off, "Poor old Kaw-liga, he never got a kiss, poor old Kaw-liga, he don't know what he missed...." And then he repeated those two lines probably twenty or thirty times.

That night when we were leaving the auditorium stage, you had to go down fifteen or twenty steps to get backstage. Lefty's wife Alice and his dad was with him. When they were going down the steps, maybe four or five from the bottom he turned and hit Alice, who was about seven months pregnant at the time, and knocked her down.

Lefty's dad told him, "Son, you shouldn't have hit Alice. You might hurt her and the baby."

I remember I was up the stairs, looking down at his daddy when he said that, and Lefty turned around and hit him.

I told him, "Mr. Frizzell, it don't take a big man to hit a pregnant woman and an old man."

He looked up at me and glared, and probably would have hit me too. But he was out of it, so he didn't.

It was one or two years before I saw him again. When I did, someone was interviewing us. They asked Lefty if he knew me.

Lefty said, "I've met Jean already." I'm sure he was referring to that time one or two years earlier.

I don't think he was a mean person; it was the liquor. I know he truly loved Alice, and I didn't think he would hit his daddy either.

Lefty and I became very good friends until the day he died. He would tell everyone that Jean Shepard was his favorite female singer. I don't think that there has ever been another male artist as great as Lefty Frizzell. There is just a small group of artists who have ever had two songs in the Top 10 at the same time. Lefty was the first one. I know Don Gibson was another one. I just don't think there will be another singer like Lefty. I am so proud and happy that I got to know him and became friends.

————

So as I was telling you, Ken Nelson was doubtful; but he did give me a contract. We had to go through a lot of stuff to get my Capitol contract in effect. Since the legal age was twenty-one, after they sent me the contract I had to take it before a judge. But the judge at first wouldn't sign it. Since he didn't know anything about the music business, he didn't know if it was a good contract or not. He gave us a couple of weeks to take the contract to somebody who could tell us. So I took it to the manager of the radio station KCOK in Tulare, California. He looked at the contract and said that it looked like a good one. So when the Capitol Records people came back to Visalia, Mother and Daddy and I signed my contract.

Jerri, the girl who played steel with the Melody Girls – when Capitol signed me she thought they wanted all of us. They all quit speaking to me real quick. There was some hard feelings. But I said, "Well I'm not going to pass up an opportunity to sing with Capitol."

Capitol called me to do my first session. I shared the billing on this record with the steel guitar player, Speedy West. My first session, as you probably know, was the "Crying Steel Guitar Waltz," and the flip side was called "Twice the Loving."

I sold about a thousand records. And I think my family bought about nine hundred of them.

I began to doubt they would ever let me record anything else again. When my contract was up at Capitol, I was convinced that that was it, I'd had my chance and it was over. I thought they were not going to sign me again.

Although it seemed like a very low point, it was really a turning point. I was at my parents' house. Mother and I at that time were taking a course on home care, studying to be nurses. I had decided if the singing wouldn't hold I could be a nurse.

Mother came and saw me laying on my bed and crying. I was laying around feeling sorry for myself because I just knew it would never happen again! Mother saw I needed to get out of that frame of mind.

My mother told me that if I don't have confidence in myself, how did I expect anyone else to.

It was probably the best advice I ever had – from a lady who only had an eighth grade education. After that, I planted my feet on solid ground and told myself that I know I can be what I want to be. I knew music was what I wanted to do. I had a taste of the music industry and this was where my heart was.

I have remembered Mother's words for the last sixty years, and I tell anybody who comes up to me and asks for advice. I tell them exactly what my mother told me.

Nobody can ever imagine what I went through the first few years. The sacrifice my parents made and the confidence they gave me – I could do what I wanted to do. I wish everyone in the world could have a mother and daddy like I did.

————

At this point, I was sharing an apartment in San Luis Obispo with Wenell, one of the other Melody Girls. We traveled and did a tour up the California coast. We'd go two or three days, then come back. By this time some men had joined the band. I was living there when Ferlin Husky looked me up to tell me that Capitol Records wanted me to record again.

I had met Ferlin twice; I knew who he was. I'd been down and done a couple little TV shows. So when he had this song he thought someone could do well with, all the guys said, "Go get Jean Shepard, she can do it." (It was probably Bill Woods, he was the one of the bunch who was my best friend. He's the one, Mother gave him my bass later on. Then he sold it. It was a Kay bass. They made brass instruments, not that many wooden instruments. So I had one of the few basses Kay made; and now I have no idea who has it!)

"A Dear John Letter" had Ferlin's attention because Fuzzy Owen and Bonnie Owens had got a lot of action on it when they recorded it a few months earlier on a Bakersfield label.

I'd been worried that I wasn't going to get another shot. But when

Ferlin came down and wanted me to take on this recording project, that changed everything. Ken Nelson came by to hear a show I was playing, at the Odd Fellows or somewhere, and from that point we began to move.

Ken Nelson also had a song he wanted me to record called "I'd Rather Die Young." It was a big hit in the pop field by a group called The Hilltoppers. Ken told me that he thought that this song would be a big one for me. "Dear John Letter" was the B-side of the record.

Naturally I was thrilled to death when we went into the studio again; it was in May 1953. Ferlin Husky was the leader of the session. The other guys were Lewis Talley (guitar), Tommy Collins (guitar), Bill Woods (piano), Fuzzy Owen (rhythm guitar), Jelly Sanders (fiddle), and Herman Snyder (bass).

In this session, when we did the "Dear John Letter," at first no one wanted to do the talking part (the male vocals are spoken, not sung). Ferlin wanted Fuzzy or Lewis to do the talking part. "If we want to get outta here," I said, "somebody better do it." Because we'd already been there three hours. So Ferlin agreed to do it.

Back then everything was recorded on monaural. This means it was like a single track, no hi-fidelity, no stereo, no nothing. Ferlin and me shared the same microphone.

————

After our first two records, we were recording in hi-fidelity. I didn't know what it meant, but I could hear it had a clearer sound. A couple years later, they told me that we were going to record on a 4-track stereo. Afterwards we went from 4-track to 8-track. Since that time we've gone to 16, to 24 – and now, they are up to I don't know how many. How can an artist use or need 64 or more tracks to make a record? I think it is dumb. Let me tell you, when you get past 8 or 16 tracks, we are getting useless. It is being overdone. Some of the producers will use so many tracks that the music will overpower the singer. I always thought if a song was worthwhile, whoever bought that record should be able to understand what I say. Ken Nelson, my wonderful friend and critic, totally agreed with me. I would never record to music that would overpower my voice. Of course it would take a lot of music to overpower my voice.

---

I've been blessed with a strong voice and have tried to take care of it. When I became a recording artist, Ken had me rest my voice between sessions; he would never let me overdo it. I would cut one session, which might consist of one or two songs. Then we'd knock off and go back the next day.

I'll tell you a good collector's item if you can find it. Capitol shipped out probably five thousand to seven thousand of these records without Ferlin's name on it. (Maybe that was why he didn't want to record with me on "Dear John" at first, 'cause he knew that would happen. They left his name off.) But after it became a hit, they tried to recall the records they had sent out. They only got back about half of them. There are a lot of 45s without Ferlin's name on it.

Four or five weeks after we recorded "Dear John," Ken Nelson got a call from a gentleman by the name of Slim Willet, an Abilene, Texas, disc jockey. (Slim later recorded and had the first hit with the song "Don't Let the Stars Get in Your Eyes.") He told Ken, "You've got a hit record with the little girl you signed." DJs were the ones who saw what was happening in the market before anyone else. In those days, DJs had power; they could play what they wanted. Slim was getting requests and playing "A Dear John Letter" about three or four times every day.

Ken started telling Slim something like, "We knew that was going to be a hit because of The Hilltoppers –", and Slim said, "I don't know what you're talking about; I mean that song with that ole boy talking."

————

So the record broke the charts in Texas due to that very special man in Abilene who made us aware of the song's popularity there. By June it was the number-one song all over. And we come to Nashville and done the *Grand Ole Opry*. It was on the charts twenty-six weeks and even high in the pop charts. Soon "A Dear John Letter" sold over a million copies.

I must insert this about Ken Nelson. When we recorded that first song, our contract called for Ferlin and me to receive one half of one percent. Afterwards, Ken Nelson went back and dated the contract to cover "A Dear John Letter" to give Ferlin and me a full one percent, which he didn't have to do. This shows the quality person that Ken Nelson was. And Mr. Glenn Wallichs, founder of Capitol Records, was also one of the finest men I knew.

————

At the time, the songwriters listed on "A Dear John Letter" were Fuzzy Owen and Lewis Talley. Now, if you look on ASCAP under songwriters, a third name is listed along with theirs. There's a story about that.

Fuzzy and Lewis heard that song first when a singer named Billy Barton showed it to them. He wanted to sell the song. Fuzzy and Lewis had nothing to trade but an old '42 or '46 DeSoto. He made the deal, and sold them his song for their car. The guys played different clubs in Bakersfield and around the San Joaquin Valley. Now they were walking to work, carrying their guitars. And Barton went around laughing at them. So me and him just never did get along.

When the song hit, Barton demanded a share of their royalties. Well he'd sold the song. They didn't owe him nothing. But he sued them to reclaim it, and the court decided in his favor. Back then you didn't get much money off a record anyway. But why give him credit?

So I never tell anybody he wrote it. And I made sure I said it to him. I told him, "I don't never tell anybody you wrote that song. You went around town bragging about making them walk to work. Laughing about what a deal you made. You done Lewis and Fuzzy real bad. I never tell nobody you wrote it." He balled up his fist. He wanted to hit me. I said, "Hit me. Right here," and pointed to my chin.

Whenever I disagree, I prefer to say it to the person directly. In many cases, that works out to make a closer friendship. But there are also people who will just get mad and hold it against me. I still think people should be direct, anyway. Gossip is more hurtful than talking to the person directly.

# CHAPTER FOUR

# ME AND THE BOYS

By August, we were going to Los Angeles to cut the follow-up to the "Dear John Letter." "Forgive Me John" made it into the Top 10; it was also in the Top 25 on the pop charts, staying on top for about ten to twelve weeks. Because of our success, it was time to travel. We had to start working the road.

Being nineteen, I could not legally travel across state lines unaccompanied by my guardian. So my mother and daddy had to go to court and designate Ferlin Husky as my legal guardian. Can you imagine having Ferlin Husky as your guardian?

Back in the '40s and '50s, you didn't go out on the road without a bunch of guys. In those days, the duet acts were hot. There was Teddy and Doyle, the Wilburn Brothers; Ira and Charlie Louvin; Sonny and Bobby, the Osborne Brothers, just to name a few. And as you have seen, the music people didn't take girl singers seriously. They didn't accept you as an artist on your own. So the women in the business at that time were always part of a duet or group. Kitty Wells worked with Johnnie and Jack, Wilma Lee worked with Stoney Cooper, and the Carters worked as a group. In that day and time, you had to work with a group or band.

On the very first trip, we stopped in Bakersfield at a restaurant. I didn't know what a clown Ferlin was. But we all sat down in this place and ordered. Well Ferlin went over to the jukebox and put some money in, and he got out in the middle of the floor and started dancing. I was so embarrassed that I slid down in the booth. I thought to myself – what has Mother and Daddy done to me, they turned me loose with this crazy man. We ended up traveling together for about one and a half years.

Working with those guys was unlike anything since. We were in music because we just loved it, and were in it together. We were like family. Separately, some of them weren't even the best musicians; but when they all came together, something tremendous happened. Together, they created a great sound. And we were true friends. Even now, to this day, if all of them were still alive (they're all gone but Fuzzy), I could say to them, I need to cut a record but ain't got no money. And they'd say, Let's go.

We had loyalty. I remember during a certain period – it got to be a joke – every time we'd start to leave Bakersfield, California, to go down to Los Angeles to record, Buck Owens would want to go with us. A lot of times I really didn't need him because Tommy Collins would be there, or someone else we knew. One time, I remember Buck was running alongside of the car and said, "Jean, you need to take me to work on those sessions."

I said, "Buck, I really don't need you."

He had ahold of the car. He said, "But Jean I really need to work on these sessions today."

"Buck, I don't need you," I said.

He would say, "Jean, please, if you don't use me today, Bonnie is going to put me in jail for non-support."

So I said, "Get in."

Buck played on a lot of my sessions. "I Learned It All from You," "I Am the Other Woman," "Act Like a Married Man," and lots more.

Looking back, people say Bakersfield wouldn't have survived without me and Ferlin's success. I didn't look at it that way. We were all just kinda kickin' around together. Then we were the ones who took off first.

Ferlin and I tried to get Ken Nelson to sign Buck to a recording contract, but he said he was just a poor man's Ray Price. I loved to hear Buck sing. But about a year later, Columbia Records got interested in Buck, and needless to say, Capitol signed him real quick. And it is all history from there.

———

Buck was so hot in the '60s and '70s – "Tiger by the Tail," "Together Again," "High as the Mountains," oh gosh, it would take me thirty minutes to name all the great Buck Owens songs.

Buck and the Buckaroos, Don Rich, and all that bunch, Doyle Holly – what a great bunch of guys. They contributed so much to our wonderful world of country music. Buck just didn't do nothing unless it was good and country. I was tickled to death when Buck Owens made it big; I knew that he would be a great country artist. I still sing a lot of the old Buck Owens songs; he wrote some of the best ever written. It was a tragic thing when we lost Buck in 2006. Not only did I lose a friend, but country music lost one heck of an entertainer and songwriter. Buck, I am glad you graduated from a sideman in sessions to a full-fledged great country music artist.

———

As I said, Ferlin and I traveled together for about one and a half years. You had to travel, because that's where the money was. Back then if you could get a thousand dollars a day, that was lucky. You went and did shows, and sold product after shows. The artist doesn't get paid for recording; the musicians do. You get paid only on sales, and you pay the musicians out of your royalties. Only if you had a big record did you make money there. Now at the time, when we would travel, my share would be a hundred dollars a night; and then I paid Ferlin fifty for my hotel and expenses. So it wasn't that much, but I had a good time. And I learned a lot.

My first royalty check was seven thousand dollars. My next check was eleven thousand and I bought my mother and daddy a home. They didn't ask me to. We found a nice place. It had three or four acres of english walnuts; you know, walnuts have always been valuable. They'd make enough in a year off just the walnuts to support them.

———

I wasn't a girl no more; suddenly I had a career and a business to take care of, men to pay their fees. It was exciting. I was interested in seeing if I could keep up with the rest of them; and I did. I held my own pretty good. I done a lot of my own record promotion. I would buy ads in the *Billboard*. And back then disc jockeys could make you or break you. Every time I had a new single come out I would order three or four hundred and send them out, one to every disc jockey on the CMA list. I'd write little notes: "Hope you like this record." I did that five or six years. I got a lot of plays from it.

We worked a lot with Red Foley, and went all over the country to record-breaking crowds. Of course, back then it only cost two or three dollars to get into a show. But the package shows were wonderful. I remember working one that was Red Foley, Ernest Tubb, Hank Thompson, T. Texas

Tyler, and Ferlin and me – you can imagine what great shows these were.

We were working I think in Montana with the T. Texas Tyler band. Paul McGee, who played drums for Hank Thompson, asked me to dance. Paul had a game leg so we could only dance slowly. The town we played had a university so there were a lot of college kids hanging around. There was a large crowd on the dance floor, and some college kids started making sly remarks like, "Hey, Blondie, why don't you dance with us?"

We tried to ignore them. Paul wasn't a very tall man but had a muscular build. I could feel him tense up and I told him not to pay any attention to them. All of a sudden, I don't know where this big, burly boy came from, but he stepped up close to us. Paul pushed me back and Dubert Dobson, the trumpet player for Hank Thompson, took ahold of my arm and pulled me out of the way. Paul drew back about eight or ten inches and hit the boy. The whole side of his face busted open. Dubert took me back to the dressing room.

Dubert said to Hank, "Got a little trouble out here. Paul and the boys are into it."

Hank said, "Who's winning?"

Dubert said, "The boys are."

It all ended within a few minutes.

––––––––

I'll tell you a funny story about Ferlin. Ferlin was one of the funniest people on the face of this earth.

We was working with Red Foley and Ernest Tubb. They told him, "Ferlin, you are running your show too long."

He was doing about twenty-five minutes and they wanted him to do about fifteen. They kept telling him that he was running too long. So one night, Ferlin got me and Tommy Williams, the fiddle player, in the car and said, "Come on, I'm going down to the drugstore." It was in Montana or someplace like that.

He went down and bought one of these great big old alarm clocks. You can hear it tick for a mile. He went onstage that night and set that alarm clock for fifteen minutes. He was right in the middle of doing his impersonations, and that alarm clock went off. He said, "Hold it, hold it, for heaven's sakes, hold it, hold it, I've got to go." He reached down and slapped the alarm off and walked off the stage.

He was always trying to get everybody to talk to Simon Crum, who was his alter ego. He got everybody talking to Simon except Ernest Tubb. Red Foley was talking to him, T. Texas Tyler was talking to him, and all of us were. Anyway we were staying at this old hotel one time, back when they had men who operated the elevator. We got into bed about four o'clock and had to get up at six o'clock that morning. Oh, man. Well Ernest had been nipping the night before, so I got on the elevator at about the seventh floor, and we went down a couple stories and picked up Ernest. The elevator guy opened up the door, and Ernest walked in. I could tell he wasn't feeling no pain. We got down to the lobby and the elevator man opened the door, and I walked out. Ernest walked out behind me, and all of a sudden he stopped and turned around and went back to the elevator and said, "Come on, Simon, get the hell out of there."

The elevator man looked around, but there was nobody in the elevator. When I told Ferlin this, he finally had his dream come true – of having everybody talking to Simon.

I wish every man and woman who has worked together or will work together in country music had the wonderful, loving friendship Ferlin and I shared for well over fifty years. Even until he passed a few years ago, our friendship was still like that. I would still call him. If I didn't reach him, I'd tell him that I better hear from him or I'd be sitting on his doorstep next morning; he would call, or have Simon call.

Oh, Ferlin, my friend, my friend, my friend.

My career owes everything to these men's friendship. During that short time Ferlin and me worked together, I got established. I will be forever grateful to those who helped me into the business. Since we started this book, Hank Thompson has passed away. I want to say, Hank, may your music live on forever, my friend. You deserve the very best that country music can give you.

———

There came a time when Ferlin and I knew it was time for him to go his way and I should go mine. The duet was waning in popularity. And Ferlin was having marital problems, which I didn't want to be involved in. And I wasn't. I always got along with Ferlin's wives (the three I got to know). Red Foley had been talking about going to Springfield, Missouri, to start up the *Ozark Jubilee*, the first network country music show. The *Jubilee* started in 1955, the same year I had a number-four single with "A Satisfied Mind." I asked Ferlin whether he was going to head to Springfield or to Nashville to try out for the *Opry*. If he decided to stay in Springfield, then I would go to Nashville.

He came to Nashville and I moved to Springfield.

———

Until I moved to Springfield, I had lived with my parents. Although I was probably gone as much as I was home, I lived primarily there. Sometimes on and off I would live with Neva Starnes in Vidor, Texas; her husband Jack was managing George Jones (and took all the money he made!). We might make a circuit through Texas, Nevada, Arizona, maybe into California. If I didn't want to go back home I'd stay with Neva.

This was probably around 1954, I guess. George didn't have his own guitar; he used to borrow my little 000-18 Martin. I knew, the first time I heard him, he was going to be a big star. It just FELT good. One day Neva called me and had booked me on several dates out through Arizona, New Mexico, and I think California. She asked if I'd be willing to pay George $50 a day to go on this trip; I said sure. The Starneses had a big western dance hall. In one end it had a little shop with jeans and western shirts. George didn't have stage clothes; he wore this old holey pair of jeans. She asked if I would get him a couple pair of Levis and a couple shirts to go on this trip, and I did. But I told him, "George, if you'd just leave off that last beer you have every night, you could buy yourself a guitar." He said, "Why? You've got one."

I was only too glad to give him the chance. Throughout that part of the country, or wherever we went, the crowds loved George. They loved him to death. Of course we all knew what a great singer he was. As far as I'm concerned, he will always be one of the best that has come down the pike.

So I had such wonderful times working those first years, and those memories are something. You know, you can't imagine all there was for me to learn when I left home and began working on the road. I never even knew that there was such a thing as gays or lesbians. We were in Portland, Oregon, and this girl came up to me and was putting her hands all over me. Ferlin called me up onstage ahead of time. He said he thought he had better get me away from her. I had never heard of that before. But he told me the facts of life that day.

Just as Ferlin had been an important friend to me, I expected working with Red Foley to be a whole new phase. I meant to stay in Springfield for a while, a couple years maybe. It was certainly wonderful working with Red Foley; to have worked with him was probably one the highlights of my career. (On down the road, one of my friendships at the *Jubilee* was going to have significance to me. That is when I met Hawkshaw Hawkins.)

Red was like a daddy to me. Me and his oldest daughter, Betty, became very dear friends, too. Red was the ultimate entertainer. He could just pick an audience up in his hand, and let them go, at will. I have seen him do this so many, many times.

It was on Red's show I first performed the song "A Satisfied Mind," which became a number-four hit. I had discovered the song more or less; I was in Springfield at KWTO's record library, just listening, trying to hear a song I liked. I would sit up at that library for hours at a time. They had a whole wall full of 45s. I run up on this; it was by Joe (Red) Hayes, who had recorded it for Starday Records. I thought, Boy that has really got a good message.

> My friends and my loved ones
> I'll leave them, no doubt.
> But one thing's for certain
> When it comes my time,
> I'll leave this old world
> With a satisfied mind.

That's a great philosophy. I listened to it, I don't know, three or four times and I copied the words down. Then I sang it on the *Ozark Jubilee*. And

Red Foley come to me and Porter Wagoner both, and said, "That's a good song. I'd like to record that."

I said, "No, I do it first and you do it next!" Or something like that.

But they both got it recorded before I did, because I had to go to California. Red and Porter both recorded it here in Nashville.

Anyway we all had hits off it. And I sold more records; because RCA and Decca didn't put out records like Capitol! It's a good record.

One night on the *Ozark Jubilee* Red wanted me to do the song "One by One" that he had recorded with Kitty Wells – which was wonderful. I told him I couldn't sing in the same key Kitty did. He insisted. Well it was just too high for me. Right at the end of it – I was so embarrassed – my voice broke. Red just put his arms around me, right on television, and he laughed and said, "Don't worry about it, sweetheart, it lets them know that you are human."

———

I truly, truly loved Red Foley for a long, long time; and to have the pleasure of working with him – nobody can imagine what a thrill it was. My husband Benny and I worked with Red years later at Ft. Wayne, Indiana, the night that he passed away. Hank Williams Jr. was with us too that night. He was about nineteen.

It was in 1968. The memory is a bittersweet one. It happened like this. Everybody knew that Red had a drinking problem. I never did drink, but Benny always had a pint of Canadian Club on the bus. Red came into my dressing room, grabbed me, and danced with me for about five minutes.

He said, "Sweetie, I haven't felt this good in ten years."

Benny said, "Red, would you like a drink?"

He said, "I appreciate that so much, but I feel so good, I don't think I want a drink."

We left that night and went on to Alabama to work for George and Lurleen Wallace; he was running for governor at that time. We checked into a motel. The next morning, we had breakfast sent to our room. Benny also asked them to send a newspaper along, and they did. Benny was laying on the bed reading the sports page. I was reading the front page, and down on the bottom right-hand corner there was a small article that read, "Singer Foley Dies." I read it and read it again, because we had just left him last night. I only knew one singer by the name of Foley. I must have lost my breath because Benny got up and said to me, "What's the matter with you?"

I was crying so hard, I just pointed to the newspaper and said, "Red Foley is dead."

He said, "He can't be, we just left him last night." But much to our sorrow, it was true.

Hank Jr. told us later that after the show that night, they stayed in a little hotel in Ft. Wayne. They went to Red's room and had a couple of drinks. They sat around and talked for a couple of hours.

Hank Jr. said when he left, Red told him, "Son, when you leave, make sure the door is locked because I think I am too tired to get off the bed and lock it."

When he went out the door, Junior looked back at Red, and Red just quietly fell back on the bed and seemed really tired. That was the way they found him. They said it was heart failure.

My years and memories with Red Foley were wonderful. He deserved more than that small article in the newspaper. Is that all he meant to the world? Shame, shame. Thank God, he meant more to me.

# CHAPTER FIVE

# THE GRAND OLE OPRY

At the same time as I was working the *Jubilee* in early 1955, I had been talking to Nashville about joining the Opry. I didn't know that they had ever considered me until November of 1955.

Back then Nashville used to host a week-long event called the Disc Jockey Convention. Later it was replaced by Fan Fair. Now it is held during the CMA Awards week, and they call it Country Music Week. The DJ Convention was held on the last week of November.

The date was November 21, 1955. Jim Denny was the manager of the *Grand Ole Opry*. We were at the Andrew Jackson Hotel on Sixth & Deaderick Street downtown in one of their conference rooms. (That historic hotel was demolished in '71 when the Tennessee Performing Arts Center was built.) Mr. Denny was making some announcements, and right at the end of one of them, I heard this:

"By the way, we would like to welcome the newest member of the Grand Ole Opry, Jean Shepard. Happy Birthday!"

I was twenty-two years old. What a way to spend my birthday! It was the most wonderful feeling in the world. I had listened to the *Grand Ole*

*Opry* on that old battery radio all those years and never dreamed that one day I would be a part of it.

Only a few years after the hit with Ferlin had changed everything, along came the Grand Ole Opry and changed it all again. Joining the Opry was a tremendous step. I had the pleasure of working with what I consider the greatest country music stars in the world. These people laid the foundation for everything that ever will be in country music. People like Webb Pierce, Carl Smith, Lefty Frizzell, Marty Robbins, Faron Young, and Jim Reeves – there was so many that I can't even begin to name them all.

I think one of the greatest pleasures was working with Cousin Minnie Pearl. I never, ever worked with Minnie that I didn't learn some little something. For instance, how to take a bow, or how to acknowledge applause better – so many little things that Minnie was such a pro at.

The Grand Ole Opry was celebrating its thirty-year anniversary during the latter part of 1955. It was the golden age of the Opry. Thank God I happened to be part of it.

———

The first night I stood on the stage of the Ryman I was scared to death. I'd heard the show all my life. Even though it was my aim I never dreamed it would happen. I remember Carl Smith was MC that night.

Carl Smith was what people would describe now as one of the studs. He was tall and handsome and could sing his butt off. He was a great stylist, like entertainers of that era could be; he had the Johnny Sibert steel guitar sound – Johnny is in the Steel Guitar Hall of Fame.

In a few years, when I eventually married Hawk, and Carl had married Goldie Hill, we were two couples the industry wasn't too happy with; but, to everyone's surprise, we had very happy marriages. Goldie was the best thing ever happened to Carl. We used to play canasta and do things like that. Goldie and Carl was expecting about the same time Hawk and I was expecting. Goldie retired to stay home with her children. I truly loved them; we remained friends down through the years. It was always such a joy to see Carl and Goldie when they would come to the *Opry*. They are gone now, but never out of mind.

My first night at the Ryman, Carl sang a couple, then me and Ferlin sang "A Dear John Letter," then they had the square dancers, and then Minnie Pearl. After Ferlin and I, the audience wanted an encore and it bothered me because they made me go back; there was only time for one so they sent me. I sang "I'd Rather Die Young."

I was at this time still cutting records for the great Capitol Record Company. At the beginning of my Opry span I was working both in Los Angeles and Nashville, with lots of touring around the rest of the USA. Joining the Opry gave us more of an outlet for our music.

It was a busy way of life, but I was young; and it was a good road to go down. I would record at Capitol's Studio A on Hollywood & Vine. In Nashville, I would sing on *The Friday Night Frolics* and work the *Opry* every chance I could get. I was still performing on the *Ozark Jubilee* in Missouri. I would tour a lot with Hap Peebles, a promoter out of Wichita, Kansas. With him we would work in the midwest, or I'd work in Texas – all over.

————

I'll tell you a few of the people I worked those tours with: I still worked some dates with Ferlin. I worked a lot with the cast of the *Ozark Jubilee*: Red Foley, and Bill Wimberly band (he was out of Texas but he worked with the Jubilee), Bobby Lord, Slim Wilson's gang (they was a band – they were great). We worked a lot back then with a gentleman named T. Texas Tyler, "the man with a million friends." Believe me, he did have a million friends. And we also worked a lot with Hank Thompson at that time.

I was meeting myself coming and going. But it was the time of my life. I was doing what I loved and had always dreamed of.

I did get tired of losing suitcases. Every time I turned around I lost a suitcase full of clothes on American Airlines. Usually it was when I was going home. It would be show suits! Custom-made by Nudie Cohn! They found a couple of them, but the last one – it was never found. I had a couple of suits made that were back then about $300 or $400 apiece. (Nudie's family continued making rhinestone stage costumes, and their suits today could run into the thousands.)

I kept San Luis Obispo airport going hot and heavy, running back and forth.

I remember one time when I had run to California just to record my album *Songs of a Love Affair*. Mr. Glenn Wallichs, the president, would always be up in his office. Glenn said he wanted to see me after I was done. When we finished up recording, I didn't have time to see him because I had to jump back on the plane to Nashville. Well a couple of days later he called me and fussed at me; he said, "I used to know a little country girl that we got along fine, and now she just doesn't have time for me." Of course I apologized and told him what happened.

———

I moved to Nashville within a few months. My first home was in East Nashville. It was on Greenland Avenue. I went out and found a nice living room and dining room set, and bought two new bedrooms sets; how exciting, to furnish my first permanent home. My coming to Nashville was a big move. I would call Mother and Daddy every week.

In 1956, after joining the Opry, I released these singles:

"I Learned It All From You"/ "This Has Been Your Life"

"You're Calling Me Sweetheart Again"/ "He Loved Me Once and He'll Love Me Again"

"Thank You Just the Same"/ "Just Give Me Love"

I had consoled myself by then to the fact that Capitol was going to be picking my songs. I was doing some songs I thought were great; Ken was always on the lookout for me a good song. Then I recorded "A Satisfied Mind." It went to number four on the country charts; it went to number one on Cashbox. That was a song I discovered. Some songs mean a lot to you and you sing them like they come straight from your heart.

"Beautiful Lies" was the flip side of "I Thought of You." It also hit number four. For some reason "Beautiful Lies" was a favorite song of half the musicians that worked for us. Robert Crigger, my piano player, boy he always liked it. It was one that fans requested all the time, too. I like the song but I had a lot I liked better.

Call me a dreamer in a fool's paradise,
My heart knows no difference that love is unwise;
Tell me you love me and will till you die;
Like music you thrill me with beautiful lies.

It tickles me to think back on working with Ken on my first album. Ken picked all the songs. He didn't want me singing songs that was a slam against me. Everything was from a woman's point of view; he didn't want me singing songs that put me in a bad light. He said, "Oh we can't have you having a love affair in a song! You're just a sweet little country girl." I said, "Ken you don't know me very well." Haha.

"We've got to keep this nice little country girl image." I chuckle thinking about him. But I was kind of naive.

----------

Maybe it was while I was in Los Angeles to record *Songs of a Love Affair* that I met Nat King Cole. I met him through Lee Gillette, a Capitol producer. Nat was in for a recording session, and Lee asked me if I wanted to meet him. I said I did. Lee and Nat were right next door to us in Studio B. Ken and I, and Johnny our engineer, went over there. There must have been forty musicians there, and half of them were fiddle players. Ken put his arm around me and said, "What do you think sweetheart?"

I said, "Look at all those fiddle players!"

Nat laughed and said, "No, dear, in Studio A they are fiddles; but in Studio B, they are violins."

And I got to meet my favorite girl singer, Kay Starr; she came into the studio.

Studio A was where Capitol's country music was recorded, and Studio B was their pop studio.

In Nashville, you know of another famous Studio B, but that was RCA. That Studio B was country. At one time it was the cutting edge. The only time I used Studio B at RCA studios in Nashville was when Hubert Long called and wanted me to do a Schlitz beer commercial. They said it paid one thousand dollars – I went directly to the studio! This man from New York handed me a sheet of music. "I don't read music," I said, and he was horrified; and Chet Atkins said, "Don't worry about it, she'll get it." There were three different commercials planned: ninety seconds, sixty seconds, and thirty seconds. Ferlin had recorded one of the commercials. So I listened to his cut for about ten minutes and was ready to cut it. We cut the ninety seconds in eighty-nine seconds, the sixty seconds in fifty-eight seconds, and the thirty-second one we had to do a couple of times to get it within thirty seconds. But within thirty to forty-five minutes, I was completely done and walked out with a one-thousand dollar check.

———

For a couple of years, say around 1956 and 1957, when Elvis Presley came into being, there was a great lull in country music. It was really hard to get your records played or even get into the studio to cut records because the world was so Elvis Presley-mad. Elvis was a really nice person and I became fairly good friends with him around 1957. I met him backstage at the Ryman. He wasn't on the show, he just dropped in. But I think they got him out there to perform.

Backstage of the Ryman they had a rocking chair. I would sit in that chair while I waited while not performing; they called it Jean's rocker. Elvis come by one night; a couple of the Jordanaires were with him: Gordon Stoker, maybe Neal Matthews, Hoyt Hawkins. Course they knew him real well. I was sitting there and they introduced me to him. He sat down and he started trying to flirt with me. He was winking. And I started laughing. And when I started laughing he started laughing. One of the Jordanaires said, "He likes you." I said, "I know." Haha. But he just fell in love with Carol Lee Cooper. She was a real pretty girl. Always was a pretty lady. He told Stoney, "I'll marry her if you'll let me take her home." But nothing ever come of it.

He dropped by there probably three times that I remember. And the first time he come he went down to a men's clothing store and bought a tuxedo. He thought he had to be dressed up. He come in, he told them, "I don't know why I dressed up."

We got Christmas cards from him for probably ten years after that. But the effect he had on the country music business was a significant new factor. Some people did one thing, some did another. Some crossed over or tried to. There wasn't much of nothing we could do, just laid back and waited. The record companies was making so much money off Elvis's records. I went almost a year without having a record released; and it hurt. It didn't seem to make much difference in our live audiences, though.

I liked Elvis, though; I really did. I think Elvis was kind of accepted into country music; because, you know, he was from the country. And he was a nice guy.

————

It was the first but not the last time that rock-and-roll would be a setback for country artists. Later it would be the Beatles.

If you'll notice, you can look up *Ozark Jubilee* and watch old episodes, and you can see that it did take on a slightly more rock influence during that time. Many artists did what they could to compete during those days and the rock influence was inevitable on country artists; some tried it. Not me. I never had no thoughts of crossing over.

————

In 1957 Ken Nelson wanted me to fly out to California and record. I asked him if the airplane tickets were coming out of my royalties and he said yes. So I told him that I wasn't coming back. Since I had been with Capitol, all my records had been cut in California. But finally I started cutting in Nashville. It is hard to remember the exact dates, but it was sometime in 1957 or 1958.

As I look back, it might have been a mistake to start cutting records in Nashville. Maybe I should have stayed with the California musicians. The musicians that I used out there were undoubtedly the greatest people I have ever worked with. Between all of those musicians, there was not one of us who could read music, literally. But when we all got into the studio, there was a sound that came together and has never been duplicated since. Some of the guys were Bill Woods, Lewis Talley, Fuzzy Owen, Johnny Cuveillo, Red Harrell, Jelly Sanders, Gene Breeden, Tommy Collins, and Buck Owens. These guys made the Jean Shepard sound and I owe them so much.

I have recorded at Bradley's Music Mill and Woodland Studios in Nashville. Most of the musicians were the same during those sessions. Guys like Grady Martin on lead guitar, Floyd Cramer on piano (Bill Pursell on the piano after Floyd got so popular), Ray Edenton on rhythm, and Walter Haynes on steel, Buddy Harman on drums, and Junior Huskey on bass guitar. Curtis McPeake played banjo along about 1962 or 1963. Hal Rugg played steel for me after Hawk's death. Wade Pepper did most of my promotional work for Capitol Records.

————

Ken Nelson would fly to Nashville to produce my sessions and would have several sessions with other singers while he was in town. Ken would bring demo records and go over the songs with me. These meetings were usually at the Andrew Jackson Hotel. He would leave the door to the room open when we were listening to the songs. He always did this, so I finally asked him, "Don't you need to close the door?"

He said something I will never forget: "Sweetheart, I always leave that door open so anyone can walk in any time, then no one will ever be able to say anything about you and me together in this room."

———

By the way, all of the unused cuts I had on Capitol were released on the Bear Family CD box set, "The Melody Ranch Girl" which came out in the summer of 1996. That set includes a hundred fifty songs or more.

For twenty years, I had a wonderful, wonderful association with Capitol Records. Even after moving to Nashville and beginning to record in Nashville, I continued with Capitol for about fifteen more years.

———

Some of the general managers of the Grand Ole Opry have really been great down through the years. There has been a couple of them who wasn't worth a toot, but we won't go into that. The first general manager of the Grand Ole Opry, of course, when I came here, was Jim Denny. He did a great job managing the Grand Ole Opry. He had a publishing company called Cedarwood Publishing Company and was very successful at that. He left the Opry in '56 and they brought in D Kilpatrick, who stayed for about three years.

The one who came after him was a gentleman that I hold so near and dear to my heart; it was a gentleman by the name of Ott Devine. They promoted him from WSM program director to Opry manager in 1959.

Ott loved the Grand Ole Opry. He truly loved his job; he loved his people. I don't care if you had a million-seller record or you hadn't sold five records, he treated everybody the same. Nowadays I think you are as hot as your last record. A lot of us don't have hot records, so we are pushed back into the corner. But Ott Devine never made that mistake.

I have such a warm spot in my heart for Ott Devine. I remember a little thing that happened. We was standing there backstage one night, and Jimmy Day, a great steel guitar player, who is long gone – but Jimmy came in and was going to play the *Opry* with Willie Nelson. Well he was wearing a pair of bermuda shorts, a tee shirt, and rubber thongs on his feet.

Ott Devine said, "What are you doing?"

Jimmy Day said, "Hey, man, I'm going to blow some steel with Willie Nelson."

"Not in that outfit you're not. You go and put on a decent pair of pants, and pair of shoes, and a shirt, and we'll talk about you playing steel guitar on the *Grand Ole Opry* with Willie Nelson."

I applaud Ott Devine. In this day and time, if Ott was running the *Grand Ole Opry*, there would not be any holes in the blue jeans, and I doubt very seriously if there would be any blue jeans on the *Grand Ole Opry*. The girls wouldn't be going out there with their mid-drifts and halter-tops on either. He thought that you should have more respect for the *Grand Ole Opry* than that. That's the reason that I always try to dress halfway decent. Ott Devine taught me a lot. When he told Jimmy Day that he couldn't play dressed like that, even though Jimmy was a great musician, Ott set a dress code, so to speak.

It is such a shame that the code is not lived up to today. If you are playing on the *Grand Ole Opry*, I think you should dress so as to set you apart from the audience. They're there to see something that distinguishes you from the everyday.

Ott Devine was a wonderful manager. He has been long since gone, but my words to him are: Thank you, Ott, you taught me a lot and I appreciate everything you did.

Jean Shepard in her Pink Dress circa 1960

THE MELODY RANCH GIRLS
L to R: CoyLou Shepard, Jerri Starling, Jean Shepard,  Francis, and Shirley

Jean Shepard's first publicity picture 1956

Jean & Hawkshaw's wedding day, Nov. 26, 1960 Whichita, KS

Jean, Donnie and Hawkshaw circa 1961

Jean, Harold and Donnie Hawkins circa 1964

Christmas Day circa 1966
Hoit, Jean, Allie Mae, Harold and Donnie

Harold, Cory, Donnie circa 1971

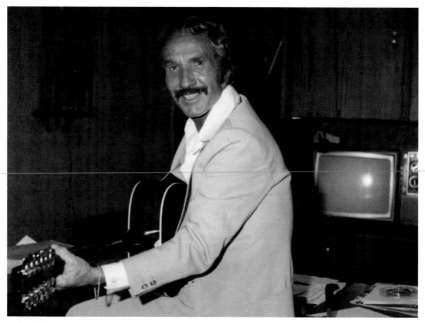

Marty Robbins

George Morgan

Red Foley

Rose Maddox

Don Gibson

Grant Turner and Minnie Pearl

Lefty Frizzel

Teddy and Doyle Wilburn

Carl and Pearl Butler

Wilma Lee and Stoney Cooper

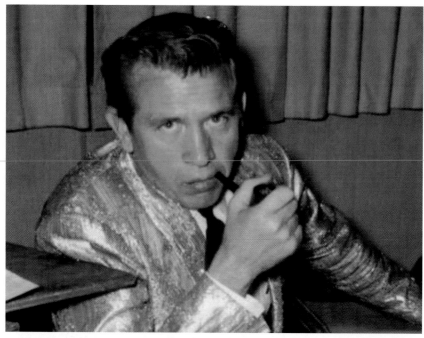

Buck Owens

Ernest Tubb and Jack Greene

"Lonzo and Oscar" pictured L to R: Oscar and Lonzo

Webb Pierce

## JEAN SHEPARD

UNITED ARTISTS

**TOP BILLING, INC.**
2000 Richard Jones Rd.
Nashville, Tennessee 37212
615 - 383-8883

To
Carl ..
one Jimmy favorite
people. Thanks for
your friendship.
Love
Jean Shepard
3-21-75

JEAN SHEPARD

A. Q. Talent Ag
903 18th Ave. S
Nashville, Tn. 3
615/329-9194

## JEAN SHEPARD

To many, Jean Shepard is simply known as "The Legend." To be called a legend in the entertainment industry one must be a pioneer and accomplish many firsts. She has done just that. She starred on the first weekly network country music show, The Ozark Jubilee, was the first female country music artist to sell a million records, the first female country artist to over-dub her voice on a record, the first to make a color TV commercial, one of the first to have her music taken aboard a space flight to the moon. She also has the longest tenure of any female member of the Grand Ole Opry -- thirty-seven years!

©1992 TENNY CARDS A DIVISION OF TENNYSON ENTERPRISES, INC.

Jean Shepard Trading Cards

Jean at the Opry

Jean and husband, Benny Birchfield

Jean Shepard and The Second Fiddles

L to R: Jimmy Yates, Eddie Payne, Jean, Benny, Jim Whitaker, Jimmy Johnston

L to R: Glen Dickerson, Dave Robbins, Robert Crigger, Benny,
Gregg Hutchins, Jean, Rick Francis

Jean and Vince Gill

Little Jimmy Dickens - "Tater"

Jean, Brad Paisley and Ruth Bauer

Minnie Pearl and Jean

Jean, Jan Howard, Jeannie Seely, Skeeter Davis

Ray Price and Jean Shepard

# JEAN SHEPARD

Smiley Wilson
Agency, Inc.
847 Springfield Highway • P.O. 1

Jean - Smiley Wilson Promo

Reba McEntire and Jean

Grandpa Jones and Jean

Kitty Wells and Jean

Jean and Roy Clark

Jean and Bill Anderson

Connie Smith and Jean

Jean on-stage at the Grand Ole Opry

Jean with Garth and Sandy Brooks

Waylon Jennings and Jean

Benny Birchfield and Roy Orbison

Harold Hawkins, Donnie Hawkins, Jean, Cory Birchfield

Jean and Mari Hart

LaQuita Alexander ( Jean's sister) and Jean

Kay Helfrich

Jean Shepard

Jan Howard and Jean

Jean Shepard and Hank Snow

Judy Mock and Jean

Jean Shepard and manager, Michael Souther, at Hall of Fame Ceremony

# JEAN SHEPARD

The Grand Lady Of The Grand Ole Opry

Bill Monroe and Jean

Chet Atkins and Jean

Jean Shepard backstage at the Opry

Gregg Allman and Jean backstage at The Ryman

Jeannie Seely, Jan Howard and Jean Shepard

Grandson, Kaleb Hawkins and Jean

Benny and granddaughter,
Icie Mae Hawkins

Granddaughter, Rachel Hawkins and Jean

Jean and Benny at The Opry Celebration , 1999

Ferlin Husky and Jean on stage at the Opry

Alan Jackson and Jean Shepard

Roy Acuff, Jean Shepard, and Ferlin Huskey

Jean at 2011 Hall of Fame Ceremony showing Medallion

Photo by Ron Harman

# HAWKSHAW

As you know, while working in Missouri I became friends with Hawkshaw Hawkins. We worked out of Springfield together, because they promoted us that way.

Hawk gave me a ride home one night, and my friend Patsy Elshire rode with us too. When we got to my place, he stopped and we talked for a few minutes. Well the next thing I knew, his wife Reva came up to the window and screamed that she had caught us. Hawk was really embarrassed. He said goodnight and I got out of the car. After that, they moved to Nashville and Hawk joined the Opry.

About a year later, I came to Nashville. After I joined the Opry, Hawk and I worked together again as a team. He was still married to Reva Barbour, who was a nice lady, but still insanely jealous – acted real crazy at times. We couldn't go out on tour together until they had a long, drawn-out, dragged-out fight. She started accusing me and Hawk of sleeping together, which wasn't true. She finally left Nashville after a while and went back to West Virginia where they were from. Their marriage ended in 1958; it had been off and on for fourteen years. Hawk was older than I was by twelve years. Him and Reva had married when they was teenagers.

Hawk was easy to work with. The audience loved him and he treated his fans good. Anything they asked him, he was all for it.

We sang together, but we didn't record together. Hawk was on RCA-Victor. Basically, no recordings exist of us singing together. There's one video, if you search YouTube, with the two of us. We were doing a show for the US Army, *Country Style USA*, where I introduced him. Earl White was on it, and Jackie Phelps. Me and Hawk didn't duet in it; but I sang one, then I introduced Hawk and he sang one, then we joined in on the chorus of the closing theme song:

> Stay all night, stay a little longer;
> Dance all night, dance a little longer;
> Kick off your shoes, throw 'em in the corner –
> Don't see why you don't stay a little longer.

There's just one other little thing on YouTube, where I'm singing "I Thought of You," and Hawk can be seen in the crowd behind me. He and Little Jimmy Dickens are side by side, along with several entertainers in the background.

After Reva left for West Virginia, Hawk and I started dating. We worked together, ate together, and rode many long miles together, so it was a friendship at first. We listened to each other's problems and cried together. I think Hawk still had a soft spot for Reva, even after we married.

Everybody thought he had a daughter with Reva. He and Reva loved Marlene and adopted her, but she wasn't their little girl. Hawk had played some dates up in Pennsylvania or Maryland or somewhere when they first saw this little girl, who was such a pretty child. Her parents literally gave her to Reva and Hawk. Now she is married with children of her own and is living in Texas.

After going together a couple of years, Hawk and I decided to get married. We were booked to go on a Hap Peebles tour, which included Topeka, Kansas. About three months before this show was to take place, Hawk had an idea he thought was great.

Hawk said, "Let's get married onstage. Hank Williams did it, so why don't we?"

So we did – on November 26, 1960, in Wichita, Kansas, on the stage of the Forum Auditorium. I really didn't want to do it that way. But an entertainer has a hard time having anything private. I went along with it, but I kind of dreaded it for those three months. But it was okay.

My dear friend Ken Nelson gave me away, Hap (the promoter) was best man, and my maid of honor was Lucille Coates, his secretary. Bill Mack owned the local country music radio station and said he would broadcast the wedding over the radio. Mark Sales was the master of ceremonies. I let them broadcast the ceremony right up until we said our vows. That part was just too personal, something that was just ours. Rusty Goodman and the Plainsmen sang at the wedding. It lasted about forty-five minutes.

Everything was furnished for us – my wedding dress, the flowers, and the cake. A lot of the big stores sent us gifts – a sewing machine and a television among other things.

But I think the best wedding gift I got was from Hawk; that being in the form of a .410 shotgun and a bird dog. Because he loved to hunt so much, he got these things for me so I could go out with him. He went to Sears and got me one of their shotguns. The first time we went hunting, he made me get on the right side of him. When you flush the birds out, they will usually fly to the right; so when I aimed my gun, I would aim away from him.

After the wedding we didn't really have a honeymoon per se. Not at first. We just came home on Bell Grimes Lane, where it was quiet. In the winters usually you get a break from the heaviest bookings. You're usually home three weeks out of four. So we had some down time after the wedding. Hawkshaw was a man's man. He liked to hunt, fish, ride horses – anything a man would do. I'd grown up somewhat of a tomboy, loving the outdoors, animals, and being active. I had a lot of energy. We were able to enjoy some of the same pastimes. And we loved to get together with friends; we would play cards and enjoy just being together.

Hawk was a lot of fun onstage. If the show got down he would always come up with some foolishness to get it back up. During our marriage, Hawk and I performed together just like we had for the previous couple of years. He added horses to the show and it was like a rodeo. They were Tennessee Walking Horses. We had one come in third at the Championship in Murfreesboro one year. In our show, Hawk had his horse, Tomahawk, perform and do tricks. There was a couple of American Indians with the show. There was Chief White Cloud who would perform with Hawk. The chief would hold a wooden box in front of him and Hawk would shoot a round into the box. Then there was Chief Red Hawk who took care of the horses. He was a very special man, but had some odd ways. He only had one tooth; and he would suck on that tooth, making a noise. He would always order the same meal: a ham and cheese sandwich to eat, and a cup of coffee.

My albums released during those years were *Lonesome Love* in 1958, *This Is Jean Shepard* ('59), and *Got You on My Mind* ('61). We recorded "Got You on My Mind" in spring of 1960. That song was one Hawk had recorded for King; and I liked the song, so I done it. I added harmony to mine. I recorded "Lonesome 7-7203" before Hawk did (Hawk's song that was number one at the time of his death). But they never released it.

Two country stars in a marriage – that is hard. Things would come up that he wanted to do and I didn't, but I'd go along with it to keep the peace. We toured together mostly. Every once in a while we would do a date separately.

Hawk and me was on this gig in Canada with Webb Pierce and Cowboy Copas. Webb and Copas went into their dressing room, which was up about eighteen to twenty big wrought-iron steps. A Canadian disc jockey came by and wanted to do an interview with Webb. Copas was sitting in the dressing room with Webb, real tipsy, sitting on his stool; both of them had had a couple of drinks. Webb was a heavy drinker.

Copas never bothered nobody. I don't know what started this conversation, or argument. But I heard this disc jockey ask Webb, "What in the world are you doing in a dressing room with this old has-been?" (He was talking about Copas.)

Webb was furious. Now Webb was a big man, weighed about two hundred pounds. We were standing in the dressing room door, looking down onto the stage. All of a sudden, Webb grabbed this man by the back of his neck and his belt, and come running out of the door of the dressing room, and was going to throw this man over the railing. It was concrete down below.

Hawk grabbed Webb and said, "Webb, don't do this! The fall will kill him."

Webb said, "I want to kill the son of a bitch! How dare him talk about one of my friends like that."

But Hawk held onto him. He wasn't going to let Webb throw him. Webb let go and he told this man. "You get the hell away from me, and stay away from me. Don't you ever talk about any of my friends like that."

Needless to say, Webb never allowed anybody to put people down in any way. I really appreciated Webb for that. To think that Webb would come to the defense of an entertainer like that only made the "family" a little closer. He grew about ten feet taller in my eyes that night.

Webb Pierce was one of the greatest country artists. Now a lot of people didn't care for his singing; he had a unique style. He had a high-pitched voice, and every once in a while onstage he would sing real sharp. People would get mad at Webb because when he went out on the stage he would strum and strum his guitar. He would do this ten or twelve times.

I asked him once, I said, "Why do you keep strumming that guitar?"

He said, "Honey, I'm tone deaf, and I have to do this so I can get the pitch in my ear."

Copas was a very underrated singer. I just remember him as a fun-loving, underrated country entertainer who didn't get what he deserved out of the industry. I loved to hear him sing. I think that he could have done rap music very well, because he did songs where he talked his way through them. That was a great gift. I admired him and truly loved him.

———

I could tell so many stories of little things I remember from our touring days together.

I hope you recall Lonzo and Oscar, a great, great comedy duo. They cut up with some of the best acts. I think their best routines were the ones when they included their "Cousin Jody" character. From backstage, I watched them over and over and over and never got tired of it.

Years ago, Lonzo and Oscar were the only ones who had a bus. There was Skeeter Davis, Lonzo and Oscar, Mel Tillis, Hawkshaw and me on that particular tour. We climbed aboard the bus to go to North Dakota,

I think. It was in February. We went about fifteen hundred miles down the road, and the heater went out. We like to froze to death. We was burning cans of Sterno inside the bus to keep warm.

Skeeter and me got into some sleeping bags and got on the bunks in the back to keep warm. Mel came back to see us; he was so cold his lips were purple. He said, "Do you have any of those things, you know those hose things?"

Skeeter said, "I have some pantyhose."

Mel said, "Give, give, give it to me." So Skeeter gave a pair to him. Do you know he put them on and wore them for three days until we got the heater fixed in that bus.

You know Mel Tillis is not only a great songwriter, but a good friend, and I love him dearly.

———

As I think of the people I've loved through the years, several I associate with my life with Hawk. Wilma Lee and Stoney Cooper is a couple who had been friends of Hawk; they had all known each other in West Virginia. When Wilma Lee and Stoney first moved to Nashville, we used to sit around in the wintertime and the four of us would play canasta. I have to say that Wilma and me would beat them unmercifully at cards.

Wilma Lee and Stoney had a very distinctive style of music. I don't know what you call it, but a lot of people call it bluegrass. A lot of people call it country music. A lot of people call it mountain music. I loved these people – not only as friends, but because they are great pioneers of our business.

When Stoney had his first heart attack, one of the first things the doctor told him was that he couldn't have sex. So needless to say it became a joke between Stoney and Hawk. Hawk kidded him about it constantly.

Hawk would tell him about his own sex life, when he knew that Stoney couldn't have any.

One time when Stoney was sick, Hawk took a chicken over to their house – a live chicken. He killed that chicken right in the garden and made Stoney a big pot of chicken soup. Down through the years, my and Hawk's friendship with Wilma Lee and Stoney was always a very bright spot. They remained friends to me all their lives.

One night down at the Ryman, Wilma Lee went on without Stoney because he was sick. I was sitting in this little room where there was a telephone. Stoney called Wilma and was talking to her, when all of a sudden he wanted to talk to me. He did a bit of drinking in his later years. So she just laughed and looked at me with a look in her eye, as if to say, Here, you talk to him. He was drunk, but I guess I talked to Stoney for about ten minutes.

After he died in 1977, Wilma Lee carried on as only Wilma Lee could do it. She was a very strong person, and I applaud her perseverance and her ability to keep on going. Her last performance at the *Opry* was at the age of eighty-nine, just a year before she passed in 2011. She was indeed a credit to the music industry. Her friendship was a true blessing. I truly loved this lady.

———

The Howards were another couple friend of ours. We became good friends when Jan and Harlan Howard first came to Nashville. Before that they had worked in California. Harlan was plugging songs to people like Ken Nelson. Both he and Jan briefly signed with Ken at Capitol, but they moved to Nashville about 1959 or '60. Hawk and me would go over to their house and play canasta. I really love Jan. Here is another example of someone who never got her dues. Jan is what I consider one of the classiest ladies that country music has ever known.

Don Gibson was another great friend of me and Hawk; as I said, our first son was named after him. Don rode to and from a lot of shows with us. I remember some really hard times that Don went through in his first marriage. I think this was the reason for Don's drug problem back then. This one night he rode back with us, and I was in the back seat asleep. We was stopping about every thirty minutes and he would get out of the car and call home to find out if his wife had gone out or was with "friends." He would come back to the car completely torn up. He told Hawk, when he thought I was asleep, that once when he called she told him don't call back because she was in bed with her lover. He was so hurt and my heart just broke for him.

Later on he married a very fine lady named Bobbi. Bobbi was one of the nicest gals that has ever been on the face of this earth. Bobbi was so good to Don and took care of him over the last thirty or so years of his life.

Over the years, Don remained a friend of ours after I married Benny Birchfield. Me and Benny went to California to work a couple dates with Don and Roy Drusky. When we pulled up in the bus, Bobbi came out and she said, "Oh, I am so glad that you are on the show with Don. He loves you so much, because you make him laugh."

What's so funny about that story was that Don never did laugh that much. He might do a little Haha, and that was it. He wrote "Oh Lonesome Me," and he wrote "Sweet Dreams;" beautiful songwriter – songs that tended to be melancholy.

Also Don had a funny side, of course. One time him and Carl Smith got into an egg throwing fight along the highway on the way to a show in Memphis. They ended up getting thrown in jail in Memphis and spent two, three weeks in jail. Don ended up having to trade in his Cadillac because of the stink.

It seems that before leaving on tour, they had bought two or three dozen of eggs and let them sit out in the sun to rot. When they got on the road, they threw eggs at each other's cars the whole trip. One would roll his window down to throw eggs at the other, and try to roll it back up before another egg could hit him. It was back when we had to roll up the car windows by hand.

They thought it was so fun they didn't stop when they got into town. Their misses started causing damage; they busted out a street light, and something else too. The Memphis police stopped them and put them in jail. That chief of police in Memphis was ready to hang them. They didn't get out till they finally got through to the governor.

Back home, Don took that car to the Cadillac dealership to trade. The salesman opened the door of the car. He stuck his head inside and sniffed. Don said, "My car don't stink."

You have never smelled such a stinking mess. They had to strip that car, carpet and all.

To me, Don Gibson was the one of a kind singer – soulful; and without a doubt one of country music's best songwriters.

These are just a few stories of the wonderful friends and memories made in those younger years.

———

Of course I was happy when we found out we were expecting our first baby. Hawk was so happy it was like somebody'd give him a million dollars. When I found out I was pregnant, I kept on working. I worked up until I was six or seven months pregnant. We had a GM 4104 bus. The travel was not uncomfortable. It was little two-lane roads, but I don't remember no trouble. I just kept going.

I'll tell you a story about a wreck we had on that bus. We had left a show somewhere up north – Pennsylvania? We were traveling along and two guys in a truck, drunk as Cooter Brown, pulled in front of us. Hawk hit them. The guy says to his friend, "Why didn't you tell me there was a car coming?" And he says, "You didn't ask if there was a bus!" It was bad. I was sore. I missed work a few weeks.

Hawk was real popular up north. You know he starred on the *Wheeling Jamboree* for years. His fan club was huge. So we did lots of shows up north. Most times we'd end up going home with his fan club people. I remember this one time after a show, we were looking for a place to make a call home. Hawk let me go in to get change for a five. Well I told the guy in the store I wanted change for a five, because I needed change for a pay phone. He just kept on asking me to repeat it. Finally Hawk come in. He said, "Where's my damn change?" I told him what was taking so long. He said, "He's just doing that to you to hear you talk." People up north used to make fun of you back then, for your accent.

Don Robin was born on December 7, 1961, and was named after Don Gibson and Marty Robbins. I had him at Baptist Hospital. (His brother was later born at Baptist, too.) Soon after Don Robin was born, we took him and introduced him onstage at the *Opry*. Hawk opened with his song. I stood there holding the baby. Then Hawk took Donnie and walked off stage and I sang my song. I've introduced most of my grandchildren on the *Opry* too.

I took about six months of maternity leave from traveling. After that we'd just bring the baby with us. I was breastfeeding, so he had to go where I went. Don Robin was a real good baby. I think our first trip with him was to Oklahoma. We went in a motor home (out on those two-lane roads).

Hawkshaw was an excellent daddy. I remember Donnie standing on the desk looking out the bay window waving at his daddy the day he left for that last trip. He was fifteen months old. Hawk went over to the Copas's house, and Copas's daughter Kathy said when she came home to take them to the airport, both men were down in the floor playing with a spinning top with one of the children.

We lived on Bell Grimes Lane off Dickerson Road. Several months after his daddy was killed, Donnie pointed to that Third National Bank on Dickerson Road – it used to be in a trailer – and he said, "I went there with my daddy." I couldn't believe that a two- or three-year-old child could remember that.

It should have lasted longer. That was about all the memories he made of his daddy.

But there came a very sad day: March 5, 1963. Kathy Copas Hughes called me about five p.m. and said that she had talked to Randy Hughes (her husband and pilot of the plane), and he had told her they were just leaving Dyersburg, Tennessee, for Nashville. Hawkshaw was on that small plane with Randy, Cowboy Copas, and Patsy Cline. The weather was not too good; and if it got bad, they would turn around and go back to Dyersburg.

About an hour after Kathy called, I put Don Robin up in the kitchen sink, pulled up a stool and gave him a bath. I was eight months pregnant with our second baby and didn't really feel all that great. But while Don Robin was having his bath, all at once the most horrible feeling came over me. It was the weirdest feeling, just awful. I felt like I was going to faint. But it passed, and I got Donnie to bed. By nine, I was worried about Hawk not being home yet. Finally I went on to bed and tried to sleep.

It was about ten-thirty or eleven when the phone rang. A woman by the name of Eileen Tait, a representative of Hawk's fan club, was calling. She asked me what was I doing. I said, "Well I was trying to go to sleep."

She started to cry and kept crying. She said, "Then you haven't heard?" And she told me the plane was missing. She kept carrying on and I couldn't hardly get her off the phone, bless her heart.

I turned on the radio and heard Tex Ritter on Ralph Emery's late night show. They said that the plane was missing. I turned on the television. The plane was missing somewhere between Dyersburg and Nashville. I called Kitty and Smiley Wilson (dear friends of ours). They came right over. The Highway Patrol searched all night till they found it about six in the morning; it had crashed just outside of Camden.

My baby doctor, Homer Pace, was the doctor to a lot of Opry stars and their families. What a precious man. He called when he heard the news. He was at my doorstep the next morning. He was really a wonderful man and was concerned about me and the baby. He didn't want me to deliver early. All my friends at the Opry came over or called me. They were really wonderful to me during this sad time in my life.

By the time I was ready to deliver, I was completely worn out. I hadn't slept since Hawk died. There were so many wonderful people, both friends and strangers, expressing their sympathy. The number of people got to me. Finally Dr. Pace restricted the visitors to just selected ones.

Mom and Dad had come. They stayed about a month after Hawk was killed. Before the baby was born I got so miserable. Daddy would say, "Come on let's go driving." And we would drive around, and I would just moan and groan. It turned out I was in labor for a week and didn't know it.

Harold Franklin Hawkins II was born on April 8, 1963, just one month after Hawk died. When Harold was born, I was both happy and sad. I knew that Hawk would never see his boys grow up.

Different friends from the Opry came to the hospital and would stay with me: Skeeter Davis, Teddy Wilburn, Jan Howard, and many, many more. Mari Hart, who helped transcribe part of this book, came by.

Hawk had three sisters (Lena and Leona are now in their eighties, but Betty has died now). His father and mother were wonderful people, just salt of the earth. I know they came, too, after his death, but it is all so hard to remember. It was a blur even then. Hawk and I had visited their home in West Virginia the two Christmases we were married, but it was really only in later years that we became close. They think our boys hung the moon.

Barbara McCool, a friend of mine, stayed with me at home for about a year. I had a hard time being the mother to Harold that I wanted to be. I would hold him, but – not long enough. It was all the pressure. It come off bad. I knew it was terrible. When he cried, I didn't know what to do. My mother would make me go sit down and she would pick him up.

———

I was so devastated for a long time. A couple of years at least – it was just rough.

Time passed. I was taking care of the two boys and trying to get back into my life. One day, I was walking into Cedarwood Publishing on Sixteenth Avenue when Marty Robbins was coming out. We stopped to talk and Marty said, "I wanted to write a song for you." He had a demo (he had recorded the song already).

I said, "You can't write a song for me because you don't know how I feel."

But he gave me the demo and I took it home and played it. Once I'd heard the song I had to admit to him, "Robbins, you did a pretty damn good job."

He had written a song called  "Two Little Boys," and he put down

Don Robin's and Hawk Jr.'s names as the writers so they would get the royalties. I thought that was the most wonderful thing to do. Marty and Hawk were real close friends.

If you see me in that *Wilburn Brothers Show* clip where I'm singing "Two Little Boys" (on YouTube), you can just almost read my face. I wasn't myself, I was just flat sad:

> Sometimes I'd quit
> If it wasn't for
> Those two little boys,
> Yours and mine....

Marty must have wrote that song for the boys and me as his own way of grieving, or it couldn't have been so true.

———

About three or four months after Hawk's death, I looked down my driveway and two or three Cadillacs were coming down the drive. It was the people who ran the Grand Ole Opry: the DeWitts, the Craigs – people from National Life. Jack DeWitt said, "We miss you at the *Opry*, and we would really like for you to come back."

I responded by saying, "I don't know if I can."

"We want you to know we want you," he told me. They said when I got ready to come on back, my job would be there. It was not like the people now, the corporate people. Last year, I was in the hospital – they didn't think to send a bouquet or give me a phone call.

So many people thought of me and either came out to the house or called. One such person was Governor Frank Clement, who was an ardent fan of country music. Everybody in this business is close, I guess, because we work in so many great shows that we became like a family.

I had decided I wasn't going to come back to the *Grand Ole Opry*. I was raising my kids. We got a settlement from Piper Comanche (the airplane company). It would have helped me over. I could have made it. The walking horse was bringing fairly good money in – enough to take care of the horses and pay the trainer. I think the house was paid off. But it meant a lot to know my job would still be waiting. I appreciated that visit and what Jack DeWitt said. I took a couple months to think it over. I loved my kids. I loved my business too. I was fully prepared to do whatever I had to do.

Finally one Saturday night, I thought I would go to the *Opry* just to test the water. I stood at the side of the stage. It was a tough situation. I went just to see if I could stand the pressure. The memories. I hadn't been on that stage without Hawk in two or three years. Believe me, friends, it was a very hard night for me.

Two or three weeks later I came back. It was hard to go onstage by myself. The audience gave a very good response; they were encouraging. They were glad I was back. I did it.

So I decided to go back to work. I called Smiley Wilson. He was my booking agent. Within six or eight months he had a dozen dates booked. Everybody was waiting to see what I was going to do. And slowly I was able to start rebuilding my life without Hawk. My friends at the *Opry*, like Goldie Hill, who was probably my best friend, and Skeeter Davis, were there for me; and Minnie Pearl would hug me.

Maybe about a year after Hawk died I bought a three hundred and five–acre farm in Columbia for my sister Quita and her husband – he was a good cattleman. I wanted some of my family near me. I wanted the boys' uncle to be close to them. So they did grow up close. Roy, LaQuita's husband, died about eight or ten years ago. The boys became close to my guitar players, too. I went to the farm about once a week when I could. And when the boys were maybe three and four years old I hired a lady to live in and take care of them (her and her daughter). But I found out she was an alcoholic, and I found out her daughter was wearing my clothes, and – that didn't work. Friends took care of them after that while I was working.

I have a photo someone took one Easter after I got the boys dressed up. They're wearing little red coats and white carnations. They were beautiful. That was before they got bigger and started fighting like cats and dogs!

Hawkshaw was only forty-one years old when he died, and was just getting his big hits. Ironically, he was on the same show that Hank Williams was supposed to be on that fateful New Year's Day in 1953, in Canton, Ohio. I don't know if Hawk announced that Hank was dead, but he did lead the singing of "I Saw the Light" that night.

Naturally, when remembering my husband's tragic death, a lot of things are hard to talk about. For one thing, so many people seem to forget that I lost a husband in the plane crash that Patsy was in. My boys lost a father. Kathy Copas lost both her husband and father. If people overlook these losses it is no fault of Patsy, and of course I honor her too. She was without a doubt one of the greatest singers that has been in country music. She was even more popular after her death. But I find it a little irritating to talk about her. I certainly don't want people to take these remarks the wrong way. I hope they will read this with an open heart and an open mind, and realize where I am coming from. I honor Patsy, I hope her songs live forever, and this comes from the heart.

Mine and Hawk's story seems glamorous to outsiders looking back on our life. But we were married just a little over two years. Think of that.

I'd just gotten used to being his wife when it was time to get used to being a widow. I was blessed with two sons with him. But our years at one another's side were short. In contrast, Benny and I are celebrating forty-five years.

# CHAPTER SEVEN

# OPRY FRIENDS ON THE ROAD

Ernest Tubb appeared in only a few of the road shows I worked while I was with Hawk. A favorite Ernest Tubb memory of mine, it was him and Hawk. This was when I worked with Ernest and rode the bus with him. We had a lot of fun on that bus. One night in Texas, in fact it was Kingsville, Texas, Hawk and me were doing a show with Ernest, and Ernest wasn't feeling any pain. When they introduced him he started to go up the steps, two steps forward, and one step back. He threw his cigarette down on the floor and kept trying to step on it with his foot, but it kept rolling away from him. He started up the steps and, as I said, he wasn't making any headway; so Hawk reached out and took his elbow to steady him and he finally got to the mike.

He started to sing "Walking the Floor over You." He sang the chorus about five times because he just couldn't remember the words. I knew then that he wasn't feeling too well.

When he came off stage, he told Hawk, "If you hadn't taken ahold of my elbow and helped me up there, they wouldn't have known that I was drunk."

One time we were parked in front of an auditorium. Ernest made a statement about the way country music was starting to change. Just then, here come a guy walking across in front of the bus toward the artists' door, and he wasn't carrying no guitar, no nothing, all he had was a hairbrush and a can of hairspray in his hand. Ernest said, "That's one of the new people."

The most memorable occasion with Ernest was in 1963. I had just come back to work, my first road trip after Hawk's death.

I was on the bus with Ernest when we had a wreck right outside Raleigh-Durham, North Carolina. A young man came down an exit ramp and hit us head on. John Wiggins was the bus driver, and I was standing up front talking with him about getting our kids in school, when this guy hit the bus. Of course everybody knows these big buses have air brakes. When the car hit us, it totaled out the front of the bus. The brakes were gone, so we had to ride it out. John was strong, and he stood up and put his foot on the brakes, but they weren't there. When the windshield busted, it made a big bang. It was like the whole world exploded. When John stood up, I grabbed his shoulders because I thought he was going through the windshield.

Ernest and all the boys were in the back of the bus playing poker. Hank Williams Jr. was on the bus with us; at this time he must have been around fourteen. His bus was behind us.

The bus finally stopped maybe ten feet from a big column holding up the overpass. Thank God we stopped, because had we hit that thing, Johnny nor me would not be alive today. I had just been in a car accident two months before, and had broken my kneecaps. Consequently, my kneecaps hit the front of the bus and broke again!

The guys came up to the front of the bus; the front door was smashed. They asked, "Jean, can you push the door open?" I said, "No, I can't."

I must have hit my face, because my nose was bleeding. Cal Smith threw his weight on the door and pushed it open. He and Leon Rhodes picked me up and set me on the road in front of the bus. Somebody got a blanket off the bus and laid me down. They didn't know if I was bleeding from my nose or mouth. Leon put a hanky over my nose and Cal put one over my mouth. They liked to have smothered me.

The strangest thing happened – some guy came up to the door and asked, "Can I help you? I am a doctor."

Cal Smith said, "Can you look at our friend?"

He said, "Sure."

He walked over and looked down at me and just turned around and walked off. He must have thought I was dead!

Somebody had called an ambulance. Johnny had broken his foot, and I couldn't stand up; so they put me on a gurney and Johnny in a wheelchair. They put us in the back of this ambulance. Nobody stayed in the back with us. They went screaming down Highway 85 to the hospital in Raleigh. We rounded a corner (this is something you would see in a comedy) and the back doors of that ambulance flew open. Johnny's wheelchair started to roll out because they hadn't fastened him down. I looked up over my head and saw this strap. So I grabbed the strap with one hand and Johnny's wheelchair with the other. We could have rolled out of the ambulance and down the street, and these guys wouldn't have known where we were.

I had to be helped in and out and up and down for about two months because of my broken kneecaps. I had two black eyes, and my nose hurt for many months. What a mess! They took me to the doctor when we got back to Nashville and tried to remove the fluid out of my kneecaps. I remember it so well because just as we walked into the doctor's office, it came over the radio that President Kennedy was killed. It was November 22, 1963.

I remember another story about Ernest. We were working in Illinois one day and I was on the show with two or three other people. The Texas Troubadours, Ernest's band, had been backing everybody; so I went on and did my bit, and the others went on and did their bit. It was getting time for Ernest to get dressed and do his show.

There was a woman who had come to the show, and she had this little baby who she had named after Ernest Tubb. She was standing down in the well of the bus, talking to Ernest. He never, ever insulted anybody or talked down to them in any way. He was such a precious person. He was wonderful. This lady kept talking and talking, and Ernest was trying to excuse himself.

He said, "Well honey, I've got to go and get dressed. It's nice talking to you. Take care of yourself."

He was just very nice to this woman. But she would not leave. She kept talking and talking, and Ernest would say, "Well honey, I've got to go and get dressed." This went on for another ten, fifteen minutes.

Finally he said, "I have GOT to go and get dressed." He said it pretty strongly, which was unusual for Ernest.

She said, "Well if that's how you feel about it, I'll just name this baby after somebody else."

He said, "Honey, I don't give a damn if you call that baby Grandpa Jones, I've got to go and get dressed."

That was just a few of the great times that I spent with Ernest Tubb. I must say, working with Ernest was some of the best times of my career.

————

Well at some point I decided to sell Hawk's walking horses. But I still kept my own horses. About eighteen months after Hawk's death, one was stolen. It was a quarter horse I'd bought from a man in Texas. So I called the police and they sent a detective named Archie Summers out to investigate the robbery. I had a good idea who took that horse. And it turned out, sure enough, the man who'd sold it to me had come in the middle of the night and walked that horse right down the driveway. They found out he was keeping it in a trailer, and I got my horse back. It was a good horse too.

But after Archie finished investigating the theft of the horse, he kept coming out to the house for some reason or another. I didn't date at all after Hawk died. I really didn't want to. But Archie kept coming by, and he certainly seemed to be a nice guy. The boys liked him and he liked them.

I did not realize at the time what a drinking problem Archie had. A dear friend tried to warn me. When I had decided to marry Archie, Tex Ritter came out to the house to see me. He put his hands on my shoulders and turned me around and said, "Sweetheart, are you sure this is what you should do?"

I think that deep down Tex knew that it was doomed to begin with. If I had only listened, it would have saved me a lot of heartaches. I told him that the boys really needed a daddy.

So we did marry. For about six months our marriage limped along, and his drinking was a major problem. Finally I told him that he needed help, maybe go to AA or talk to our minister. So the minister came out to the house to talk to us together. But Archie just didn't take any advice from anybody.

I had to do a show in Canada, so I told Archie that while I was gone, he should move out. I was playing at the Horse Shoe Club in Toronto. I'd gotten to know a lot of the law enforcement guys up there, especially a detective from the city police department. Archie called and told this detective that he was going to surprise me. When he got off the airplane drunk, this detective took Archie out to dinner, and they had a few more drinks. When they finally came to the show, I could have crawled under the stage. The next morning, I told him he had to go back to Nashville, and don't be in the house when I get back.

Before he left Toronto, he told me he would change. So I said we would try again. But by the time he got off the plane in Nashville, he was drinking again. That was it! It was over.

Archie's brother had been living with us and my niece was staying with us too. I went to the *Opry* one Friday night, and when I got home my niece was all upset. I asked her what in the world was wrong. She told me that Archie's brother tried to rape her. Well I just lost it. Archie made him leave.

I really liked Archie's dad. But his mother, who had been put in Central State, a psychiatric hospital, called me up on the following Tuesday or Wednesday saying I was telling lies on her son. But I knew my niece and what a good girl she was. Archie's mother was a very sick lady. She had told me once that she had a butcher knife that would fit my throat. One time she tried to kill one of her children. Her husband called her doctor and finally had her committed. I never did see her again.

Once when I was in the kitchen, a bottle of whiskey fell out of the cupboard and hit me in the head.

You know, I tried to make our marriage work; but it was over for good.

———

Tex Ritter had tried to warn me about Archie. Don't you love friends who look out for your best interests? Let me tell you about Tex.

I know everybody gets tired of my saying throughout the book that I love this person or I love that person. But it is so true, and the wonderful memories that I have of these people – I wouldn't take a million dollars for them.  To think that I got to work with all these great artists who made the country music industry what it is; believe me, I consider it a feather in my hat. I have a heart full of memories.

Tex was one of a kind. Even now, you go and see the old movies, like *High Noon* with Gary Cooper, and the wonderful voice of Tex singing "High Noon" will never be forgotten. I loved to be around him because he had such a great sense of humor.

I know a lot of funny stories about Tex. One time he was planning to go overseas and needed to have this shot. He didn't want to take it, but he did anyway. He went down to the health department and the nurse told him to drop his drawers. So he dropped his pants, and she gave him the shot.

He said to the nurse, "Sweethaarrrt, just in case you don't know it, you just gave a shot in the ass to America's Most Beloved Cowboy."

Back then there was a lot of hijacking planes. Well his plane got hijacked to Cuba, and it took him three days to get home. He was a total wreck!

He made a run for senate one time. His wife, Dorothy, was a precious lady. She thought he should walk along the streets of small towns and go into the businesses and introduce himself.  They said every place they would go in, like a hardware store or gas station or something, Dorothy would buy something because she figured that she should, and they ended up with a hundred and fifty cases of motor oil and a bushel basket of screwdrivers and hammers!

I worked many dates with Tex and enjoyed every one of them. I hope for the next fifty years, I can turn my television on and watch my dear, wonderful friend Tex Ritter sing and ride that white horse across the screen. Aren't memories wonderful?

My memories from that part of my life would fill many chapters.

I would never get tired of telling you about those people I was getting to know and love through my Opry association.

Carl and Pearl Butler was a man and wife team. I truly loved Pearl. Carl was very hard to love; he was just a "hardball" kind of person, but I liked him okay. He was hard to get along with, and Pearl was always the peacemaker. Carl would hack somebody off and Pearl would come along and try to smooth things over. Sometimes it became hard to forgive Carl for some of the remarks that he made. They did have a very distinct style. When you hear their records, you know immediately who is singing. They both are gone now; and after all is said and done, I will always be a fan of theirs.

————

Here's another Opry friend who started with Capitol in California, Martha Carson; I think I knew her since forever. Martha was a redheaded fireball. She was known mostly for her gospel influence in the music industry. But I think she could have sang anything she wanted to. At one time, her husband, X Cossee, tried to get her to sing some pop songs; it just didn't fit Martha, because her heart and soul was in country and gospel. When she passed away about ten years ago, this redhead bombshell left her mark on all of us.

————

Jim Reeves, of course, I worked with at the *Opry* and on the road. He was a pleasure to work with as much as a pleasure to listen to. He probably had the smoothest voice in country music. Sometimes I think that Jim sang too good. He is just as popular today as when he was alive. Nobody could say anything bad about Jim Reeves. (Because he'd probably sock them in the nose.)

One of my most treasured memories: I remember one time on the road with Jim, after the show was over, it was still early. Some of us, we went down to a bowling alley and bowled two or three games that night. Jim didn't go, but two or three of his guys were there. Dean Manuel, his manager, told me, "I don't think you know how much Jim likes you. Jim Reeves thinks you are the best country girl singer in the business. Always there and you are always right on it." It meant a lot to me coming from him.

The next day, Jim came by and I mentioned it to him. He said, "Your music is right on it."

The way he died, of course, brought back painful memories. He and Dean Manuel died in a plane crash in 1964. It was one of the saddest things. His music is greater now than before. Thanks Jim, for your support and your wonderful music; I treasure them.

———

You would enjoy knowing how I met a fan who grew to be one of the *Opry*'s beloved entertainers: Jeannie Seely. The first time we met, I was probably twenty, and she was waiting in line to get my autograph. I had done this show in her home state of Pennsylvania at a place called Hillbilly Park. She was about fourteen years old and she had bought one of my pictures and she was just standing there and staring at me. I thought, "What's wrong with this girl?"

Finally I looked at her and said, "You want me to sign that picture?" She said, "Yes."

I said, "Well then ask me!"

She joined the Opry about ten years after I did. They call her "Miss Country Soul," and the name fits her very well. She has a husky sounding voice and it became a great style for her. But I can always picture the meek and patient young girl.

Then I have a special place in my heart for The Willis Brothers: Guy, Skeeter, and Vic. What a trio! Not only were they wonderful musicians but they were from Oklahoma and I'm from Oklahoma, so that made them extra special to me.

I rode to several show dates with them. They would stop every thirty miles and ask for directions. I don't think they could follow a road map. We would drive four hundred miles and we would stop about six times asking for directions. They were just a funny bunch of guys.

In '74 we moved down here to the new Opry building and they gave us lockers, which we never had before. So Vic said, "Boy, these are big lockers. Man, you could get your fiddle and your guitar in there." Well Billy Grammer's wife, Ruth, was standing there with Vic.

He stepped up beside his locker and said, "Ruth, get in here with me and show them how big it is."

So she stepped up and into the locker with him. Of course their knees were kind of buckled down; they pulled the door to and it locked. Nobody had the key. So they had to go get Mr. Van Dame or Mr. Bell, the guards, who had a master key. They were in there for about ten or fifteen minutes, and when they unlocked that locker, they couldn't hardly get out of it because their knees were so bent up. What a crew this was.

Let me tell you something, there have been many people on the *Grand Ole Opry* who have been wonderful hosts or hostesses (who MC the show). You have never been introduced right until you were introduced by Guy Willis. He was the best that has ever been. He would make that audience think that Queen Elizabeth or the president was coming out there to entertain. He made them believe it. My hat is off to these wonderful, wonderful guys.

I worked with The Willis Brothers one time down in Florida, and

Carl Perkins and his bunch was on the show with us. I only had a guitar player. This was many years ago, and with me was guitarist Billy Byrd, who used to play with Ernest Tubb. Well everybody knew that Billy had a drinking problem, but he stayed pretty straight with me. He really did, in all sincerity. But he got down there with Carl Perkins and his brothers and they got into the moonshine or whatever. So we went out on the stage and Billy Byrd couldn't find his rear end with both hands. So The Willis Brothers, who were great professionals, walked out there behind me. Billy Linneman was playing bass, Guy played rhythm guitar, Skeeter played fiddle, and Vic had his accordion. Now Billy Byrd wasn't hitting nothing, so Skeeter took his fiddle bow and kept tapping the volume control on Byrd's amplifier. He would tap that little knob and finally turned it completely off. They stood up there and you thought it was all a part of the show. That's how great they were.

———

I should tell you a few things I remember about Hank Snow. Back when there was no such thing as motels, we stayed at hotels. It was Hank Snow, Slim Whitman, and me on this particular show. After the show ended, I went back to the hotel. I was laying on the bed reading when I heard this party getting started down the hall. I could hear the glasses clinking and everyone laughing. I thought there was going to be a drinking party that would keep me up all night.

About an hour or two later, I heard a woman screaming at the top of her lungs. I thought, Oh my God, there is going to be a murder and I am going to be a witness.

So I opened the door with the chain on it, and I looked down the hall. Here comes this woman. All she had on was a bra and half-slip, and had this thing in her hand, holding it up above her head. She was looking at it and screaming at the top of her lungs. Now right behind her came Hank Snow. He was wearing only a pair of boxer shorts that came down to his knees. He came up behind the woman, taking little steps and pointing his fingers up, trying to get what she had. It took me about five minutes to realize that she had his toupee in her hand, and he was trying to get it back. I got down on the floor and laughed until I almost wet my britches.

We was coming home from I don't know where, but it was the Wilburn Brothers, Hank Snow, and me. We stopped outside of Memphis, Tennessee, at this little restaurant. Hank Snow had been drunk the night before and still wasn't feeling no pain. So we ordered some food. The waitress was very nice and very pretty. Hank kept calling her "honey" and "sweetheart" and all these nice names.

There was this big man sitting in the corner booth, weighing about two hundred and twenty pounds. For about twenty minutes Hank kept talking like this, till this big guy walked over to him and said, "That is my wife and I would appreciate you not calling her all of those sugary names."

Once we worked in Denver, Colorado, and Hubert Long, who used to manage Webb Pierce, Faron Young, and so many others, was at this particular show. I loved Hubert Long; he was a wonderful man. Hank Snow, Faron Young, Webb Pierce, and me was on this show.

I had checked out of the hotel and went to the airport to meet Hubert Long. Here comes Hank and Webb right behind us, and they were so drunk. We didn't want to be seen with them. So we got on the plane first and went right to the back of the plane, sat as far back as we could. Hubert put the newspaper in front of both of us so they couldn't see us. There was only eight or ten people on the plane.

Back then, if you smelled of liquor they just wouldn't let you on the airplane. Webb had this flask with some liquor in it. The stewardess asked them two or three times to put the flask away. She said, "You are not supposed to have it on the plane, and we could get into trouble by letting you on drunk."

I saw this stewardess go to the back of the plane and she picked up the phone. I could tell she was talking to the pilot. A few minutes later, the cabin door opened and out walked the biggest man I had ever seen – he must have been seven feet tall.

He walked over to Webb and Hank and said to them very softly, "Sir, you are giving our stewardess a hard time, so I am going to ask you to put that flask away. Sir, if you don't do what I ask, Sir, I am going to unscrew your head, shit in it, and then screw it back on."

They settled down and within five minutes they were asleep. I'm going to guess that would have been in the early '60s. Of course Hank Snow was a senior member of the Opry when I was coming up, so our careers overlapped from the '50s till his death in 1999. At the other end of the spectrum, here's a character I can tell you about from the time he was toddling backstage with his mother: Hank Williams Jr.

Audrey, Slim Whitman, and I were working a series of shows, so I got to travel with Audrey quite a bit. This was in the mid-50s because I remember Hank Jr. was about five years old. One night in Albuquerque, Audrey asked me to keep an eye on him while she performed. So I said sure.

I was wearing some real pretty silver high heels. That pup marched right over and stomped on one of them. He was wearing little cowboy boots. I said, "Boy that'll get your butt busted."

Well he looked up at me and stomped on the other shoe. I grabbed him and batted his butt a couple times.

When Audrey came off the stage, she said, "Was he good?"

Hank piped up and said, "She hit me!"

When she found out why, she just sorta said, "Well son you shouldn't do that." She didn't ask me to watch him no more.

———

So that was one of many lifetime friendships that dates back from my early Opry years. Another, of course, is Marty Robbins. Although he later became Hawk's close friend, I first met Marty in 1951; this was the year he joined the Opry. I had the pleasure of working with him in California. Just listening to him that one night, I knew that he was destined to be one of the greatest voices that country music has ever known.

I am a big Marty Robbins fan to this day. I love his cowboy songs. I was playing Marty Robbins at home one time when my granddaughter Icie was about six years old, and she just started crying. She was listening to "Big Iron." And she said, "I want to see Marty Robbins." I said, "Honey, he's gone to be with Jesus." But she told me she wanted to see him. And she just cried.

After I joined the Opry, Hawk and Marty became very, very good friends. They did a lot of things together – horses, hunting, racing. They raced those little micromidget race cars together.

When we used to do the *Opry* pre-show, *The Friday Night Frolics*, from the WSM radio station at Seventh and Union, you never knew what was going to come out of Marty or Hawk. At that time, for some reason or another, Marty did not like to use a fiddle. I think he used a fiddle later on. Anyway, Hawk played just enough fiddle to irritate Marty. Marty would be singing and Hawk would pick up Tommy Jackson's fiddle, walk up behind Marty and start playing this squeaky fiddle. Well, Marty would just about come unglued. Now Hawk didn't like the mandolin. I think he got that from me. When Hawk would sing, Marty would pick up the mandolin and start to play and do the same thing to Hawk. It got to be a riot.

One night at *The Friday Night Frolics*, about one month after Don Robin was born, I looked down and my blouse had become very wet, even though I had on nursing pads to take care of this. I didn't know what I was going to do. I had on a green dress and Marty had on a bright red cardigan sweater.

He said, "Here, Mama, you better put this on."

I wore his sweater that night and he sat there until we got off the air. He walked us to the car and I gave it back to him. I don't know what I would have done if he hadn't given me his sweater to wear.

A few years later when I married Benny, not many of my country music friends approved of him. A lot of them kind of shut me out, so to speak, and Marty was one of them. But the last year or so that Marty lived, he began coming around. Not long before he went into the hospital for the last time, he came into dressing room twelve at the Opry. He had been there a couple of times before just to chat with us. But on this particular night, he came in and sat up on the sink with Benny and we all sang several songs together.

I said to him, "Are you slumming tonight, or are you just lonesome?"

He kind of laughed and said, "Well a little bit of both."

———

Another of my friends who had been a friend to Hawk was Faron Young. He made his start on *Louisiana Hayride* in 1951, and the next year he joined the Opry.

I am trying to write the truth as I know it, and not what people were made to believe; well, with Faron that is going to be hard. But I will try. I truly loved Faron Young. I loved him for his outspoken nature – because I have tried to be the same way down through the years.

Faron was a fellow artist at Capitol Records for many years. They called him and me in one time to make a record for the sponsor, Pillsbury Flour. You could use a coupon in the bag of flour to buy a little EP with two songs on each side. I put "Be Honest with Me" and another song on my side. Faron did two songs for the other side. So Hawkshaw dropped me off at the studio and said he would be back in an hour or so. I did my songs and was fixing to leave when Faron came in with a bottle of beer in his hand. He asked me if I wanted a drink and I said, "Faron, you know I don't drink." He was pretty high.

He said, "You think you are too damn good to drink with The Sheriff?" (People called him that after he acted in a western movie, and afterwards he named his band the Country Deputies.)

I said, "No, but I don't drink with anybody."

Faron grabbed me on the back of my neck and pushed this beer up to my mouth, and the beer was spilling all over me. I was just mortified when I went outside where Hawk was waiting. Since Hawk never drank, he could really smell that beer.

He said, "Have you been drinking?"

I said, "You know better than that."

I didn't want to tell him the whole story because I knew there would be some serious problems between Faron and Hawk. Hawk just kept going on and on because he could smell the beer on me. After we got almost home, I told him what happened. He got furious. The next week at the *Opry*, Faron walked by and Hawk grabbed him by the front of his shirt. Now as most people know, Hawk was six feet, six inches tall and weighed about two hundred pounds. He literally lifted Faron off the floor. And Hawk didn't pull any punches.

"Let me tell you something you son of a bitch, don't you ever do anything like that to my wife again. I respect your wife and would never do anything to her like that, so I expect you to pay my wife the same respect."

Bill Carlisle walked by and said, "Hit him, Hawk, hit him."

Faron was married to a lady by the name of Hilda, a very, very sweet lady. She was one of my personal friends. She came into the hospital when my first baby was born and brought a beautiful box of chocolates. I was nursing the baby and I ate two or three pieces of chocolate. I guess it didn't do the baby much good; it upset his stomach and gave him diarrhea. So the nurse threw the beautiful chocolates away. Hilda was sweet. I thanked her for the gift.

Everybody knows Faron had a drinking problem, of course. After Hawk died, I worked a date with Faron in Michigan, and Faron was drinking. He came up to me after the show was over and told me that I needed to go out with him. He said that Hawk wouldn't care. He and Hilda were separated at this time.

This really upset me. At this point in time, I was not ready to start dating; and even if I had been, I would never go out with anybody in the music industry. But I remember my reply to Faron because I was so upset. I said, "Faron, if and when I decide to go out, I will find a real man."

Needless to say, Faron got very ticked off at me. But it didn't last long.

I'd like to say this about Faron Young – when he was on a roll, he was probably one of the best entertainers that country music ever had.

Once we worked with Faron in Florence, Kentucky, on a show with Grandpa Jones, Pee Wee King, and Redd Stewart. This was after I was married to Benny. The people who ran the show asked me and Benny how we should line the people up. We knew they had a bar there, and we knew how Faron was.

At that time, Grandpa Jones was really hot because of the *Hee Haw* television show. I told the promoter to let Grandpa close the show.

I said, "Let me go on, then Pee Wee King and Redd Stewart, then Faron Young; then let Grandpa Jones close the show."

They said, "We want Faron Young to close the show."

Well we had three shows to do, and the first two went real good. Then the third show, Faron was really out of it. It was a Fraternal Order of Police show, and Faron got into a fight with some of the policemen. It was a disaster.

When we got back to Nashville, I went down to Billy Deaton's office. Billy had been Faron's manager for years and years. Faron was right there, and I told him, "I don't ever want to work with you again!"

I said, "Faron, you need to realize one thing, you are a drunk. You are an alcoholic. You need help." He didn't say too much.

Later on that afternoon, my phone rang and it was Vic Willis. He said, "Jean, have you talked to Faron today?" I said, "Why?"

Vic had an office downtown, and Faron had come by the office and told him, "I need help. I am an alcoholic, and I didn't realize it until someone I love very much told me so." After that Faron went on the wagon for quite a while.

Faron was one of the kindest people that you would ever want to know. He was a good person. If I wanted something, he would say, When do you want it?

About a year or so before Faron died, we did a show together. They had a little trailer for us to dress in and they put food in there for us. Me and Benny and Faron sat in this little trailer most of the day. We laughed and told what we called war stories, like I am telling you now. It was one of the nicest days we had had in years.

I told Faron when we got ready to leave that day, I said, "This has been one of the greatest days that I've had in years. It has been so much fun working with you today – like old times. I want you to know that I just love you to death."

He put his arms around me and said, "Hell, Shep, you know how much I love you."

Nobody liked him when he was drinking, but everyone grieved at his death in 1996, which was such a tragedy. The world lost a good entertainer when Faron took his life. As far as I am concerned, he recorded some of the greatest songs that have ever been recorded in country music. I would like to salute Faron Young for his contributions to our industry.

———

Well. Why don't I tell you a few funny stories and not end this chapter on a tragic note. A guitarist I've known for years told me this the other night before I went onstage at the *Opry*. I've heard this story before. He said one night Faron Young and Mel Tillis was over at Tootsie's, the famous country music bar down by the Ryman, and the two of them got into a fight. Now I mean they was fighting. Finally Mel got Faron down on the floor, and he put his foot on Faron's neck, and he held him there and he said to him, "Take that Old G-g-golden Throat!"

Mel Tillis is a character, I'll tell you. We don't have hardly any characters around here any more.

Porter told us a story on Mel; they used to be big fishing buddies for years and years. Now Porter could catch a fish in a radiator. Mel and Porter's fishing hole was up on Center Hill Lake, about seventy miles from Nashville.

This one day Porter picked Mel up in his new Cadillac, and they began driving to the lake. Well as they were riding along, Mel kept on breaking wind. Porter told Mel to quit breaking wind in this new car. So they went along; well, Mel broke wind a few times. Porter said it was so terrible that it would gag a maggot. Finally Mel lifted up his hip to break wind, and he crapped in his britches!

He said, "Oh, oh, I – I – I messed all over myself."

He told Porter to find a gas station that had a restroom on the side of the building so he could get out of the car and slide into the rest room and clean himself up.

Porter said, "You SOB, I'm not going to stop, and you will get out of the car when I do stop."

When they finally stopped, Mel got out and slid along the side of the building. He took off his pants and washed them out. He got back into the car. Evidently, Porter had cloth seats in the car and it left such a horrible odor. I'm sorry I had to tell this one, but I know it's true because Porter told me.

Here's another fishing story. One night they was in Porter's boat, and as it got darker you could see the Northern Lights on the horizon. You know, when the atmosphere is just right, every once in a while you can see the Northern Lights.

Well, so Mel got real upset; he said, "The Lord's coming!" He started throwing beer overboard; he said, "The Lord's coming! We've got to get rid of all this beer and these cigarettes!" Porter said, "Don't you think the Lord knows you been smoking and drinking?"

Porter said Mel didn't tell him he was going home, but he just got out and that's what he did. Mel got in his car and he drove all the way home. Porter couldn't get him on the phone for three days. Mel wouldn't pick up the phone. Finally on the third day, Mel answered the phone. Porter lowered his voice and said, "Mel, this is Jesus." Mel quickly hung up the phone.

———————

About twenty years back, when our grandson Robin was about six, he was playing around backstage during the *Opry* and he come to my dressing room with his hands cupped full of rhinestones. He said, "Look what I found!"

Benny said, "Where'd you get those?"

Robin said, "In the men's room. There was a trail of them all the way to Porter Wagoner's dressing room!"

# CHAPTER EIGHT

# LIFE WITH BENNY

Late in 1966, I think, during the old DJ Convention at the Andrew Jackson Hotel, I was visiting with people in the Capitol Record Company's hospitality suite. That's the first time I remember seeing Benny Birchfield; he was singing with the Osborne Brothers at the time. He sang with them for ten or twelve years.

I could not have guessed he would become the partner I would complete the rest of my life with. But he did make a fine first impression. He was a good singer and a good picker, and had a lot of personality, a real storyteller. He could be very funny and also very wise. We just sat around talking, and I thought, Well he's a nice guy.

Later, when I worked some dates with the Osborne Brothers, Benny and I would get to talking. He told me he was from Isaban, West Virginia. When he was younger, with his first wife, he had four kids, and then from his second marriage he had two kids. I had my two boys by Hawk. So we spent a lot of time talking about our kids. We had a lot in common in that respect.

Eventually Benny left the Osborne Brothers and came to work for me as my front man. He is so talented on the guitar and banjo, and a true lover of bluegrass. As we continued working together and getting to know each other, I saw he was a nice somebody to sit down and talk to. And it picked up from there. It is hard to say exactly when I knew this was love. I liked so many things about him. I know one thing we both agreed on: that this new stuff we were hearing was not country music.

We had spent about two or three years working together and had grown to love one another; one day Benny came over and said, "Let's just go and get married." So I put on a dress and off we went to Gallatin, Tennessee. We took a blood test and they gave us an exam; it cost twenty-five dollars apiece. While we waited for the blood test, I went up to this little boutique on Main Street in Gallatin and found this coat for about forty dollars. I wrote a check for the coat. When we went across the street to the courthouse and picked up the license, I had written the last check in my checkbook. Benny only had about two dollars on him, and I didn't have a dime on me, so we had to drive all the way back to Hendersonville, get some checks, and then drive back to Gallatin.

It was November 21, 1968. If you're paying attention that date should ring a bell. It was my thirty-fifth birthday, my thirteen-year Opry anniversary, and now my wedding anniversary. I would jokingly say, And it's all been downhill ever since! But I guess I can't say that; it's been forty-five years now – I think it's going to last.

We didn't go on a honeymoon at that time, but probably fifty times we've gone a week away somewhere and we say it's our honeymoon. We're still on our honeymoon. We have a good time together. We solve all the world's problems riding along in a car. Course they don't none of them get solved, but....

We had such a great time, right from the first. A lot of the things we did together of course involved the children. We would go to Center Hill Lake. A lot of us used to fish up there: Jerry Reed and Mel Tillis and Porter, just a whole bunch of people. Me and Benny used to have a boat and a little cabin up there, and if we had a week off we'd go up there a few days just to get away from it. The cabin was eighty miles from here. It's a pretty drive, and it's just one of the most beautiful lakes you can imagine. We haven't been up there in about ten or fifteen years. I hope it hasn't changed. Small mouth, large mouth – we'd catch anything we could. We just went mostly for the relaxation on the water and the boat ride.

Or sometimes we played baseball with Sonny Osborne and his family. It was his family against our family. He had a couple kids and we had a couple kids; we played baseball a lot. We've got several little baseball fields here around Hendersonville for the kids to play ball.

Of course, we also worked quite a schedule. And let me tell you, if you're going to be a working mother you better have a good babysitter. And I did. We were gone twenty days a month – sometimes a little more, sometimes a little less. Music is a full-time job.

But whenever possible we would take time for friends and family, sometimes even while on the road. You remember I had a younger brother named after my daddy: Hoit, who we called Sonny. He's the next younger one after me. One time me and Benny went out to California – my God, it has been about forty years ago now. Sonny would work a few little beer joints around there, just for the fun of it. They had this steel guitar player, Jay McDonald, who used to play with Buck and a bunch of them. Hoit said, "Why don't you all come down. Jay is playing steel."

So we went down to this little club, and Sonny got up to sing. I sat there with my mouth hung open. I thought, Why haven't you been doing this all along?

I told him, "Sonny, let me get you a recording contract."

I was still with Capitol Records at that time, so it was around 1970.

He said, "Sis, I don't want to make any records, I just like to get up and sing."

But I tell you he sang his butt off. Good country music, I'm telling you. It just blew my mind. But he just didn't want to go any further with it.

———

Through Benny I came to have a greater appreciation of bluegrass artists. I always liked bluegrass music, but until then I never had studied it. Of course I love the Osborne Brothers. Nobody can sing bluegrass harmony like Sonny and Bobby Osborne and my husband. The harmony that these guys shared – nobody can come close to it. As far as I'm concerned, when Benny sang with them, it was the best they had. Sonny has retired, but Bobby is still out there going strong. We love you guys.

Lester Flatt and Earl Scruggs, as you know, were just legendary. When anybody mentions bluegrass, I automatically think of Lester Flatt and Earl Scruggs.

We was a lot closer to Lester Flatt than we was Earl Scruggs. Him and Benny was really good friends. I had a little GMC 4106 bus. Lester had a Silver Eagle, which was a bigger bus. When Lester began to slow down and was gonna more or less quit the business because of illness, in the late '70s, I got his bus. He took ours and gave us his Silver Eagle. He gave it to us, more or less. I know that Vern Gosden had offered him thirty thousand more for that bus than I could pay. But I think he just wanted us to have his bus. He said, "No I'm going to let Ms. Jean have my bus." I know he took a hit on it. We loved Lester and Earl, and I think they loved us too.

Springer Mountain Farms Chicken was presenting the Thursday night *Bluegrass Night* at the Ryman, maybe two or three years ago. I had the pleasure of watching Earl Scruggs, and he was tremendous. Oh, it was just a magical night. The only thing that was missing was Lester Flatt stepping in and saying, "That's got 'em Earl."

They sang the *Grand Ole Opry* Martha White theme for so many years:

Now, You bake right with Martha White,
Goodness gracious, good and light, Martha White.

Now the *Opry* has Rhonda Vincent singing it. What a shame that the *Grand Ole Opry* and the Martha White people let Lester Flatt and Earl Scruggs' theme song get away from them. Shame on you people!! That was a classic my friends, and we will always miss it at the *Grand Ole Opry*.

Mac Wiseman is another bluegrass artist I've come to love. He can sing country, or he can sing anything; many people consider him bluegrass and he's a member of the Bluegrass Hall of Fame. This man can flat sing. He sings with such feeling. He has a passion for his music.

One story comes to mind. We were in Belfast, Ireland. One night after a show, this big guy came into our dressing room and asked if we were Jean Shepard and Benny Birchfield. We said yes we were.

He said, "Well I am Chief of Police So-and-So, the chief of police of Belfast."

He looked and sounded so mean. I thought to myself, Oh God, we are in a lot of trouble now.

He said, "Let me tell you something, Mac Wiseman told me that if I don't take care of you when you are here, he was going to kick my ass."

Another story, we were working with Mac a few years ago and we said, "Let's go out to dinner sometime."

He said, "Yeah, give me your phone number and I'll call, and me and my wife will go out with you."

Well we never did do it. This went on for years.

So what I done, I filled out a musicians' union contract and I sent it to Mac saying that Benny and me and Mac and his wife would meet at the Peddlers Restaurant on such and such a day. The ones that don't show up will pay double when we do meet. I mailed it to Mac, and he signed it and sent it back. We finally went out to dinner. I love you, my friend.

———

Jim and Jesse McReynolds – another of the bluegrass groups I've known down through the years. Two brothers – just sang their butts off, and just played the music like it should be played. We lost Jim a few years back, but we're glad we still have Jesse here at the *Grand Ole Opry* keeping their music going. Keep it up Jesse!!

Needless to say I also loved Bill Monroe, and I'm saving a funny story about Bill for a later chapter.

———

When Benny and I had been married for a little over a year, we became the parents of a son, Corey Howard Birchfield. Corey was born on December 23, 1969. With my Harold and Donnie, plus Benny's six, our new baby brought it to a total of nine kids. Then Jamie Hall, a close friend of one of our boys, began hanging around all the time. He slowly became a part of the family and is like a son to me. He stayed four or five years. So we claim a total of ten kids, twenty-seven grandchildren, and two great-grandchildren.

I have six step-children. First is Donna, the oldest one, and the only girl that we have; then there is Don, an entrepreneur of all sorts; then we have David, Ronnie, Benny, and Greg. That's my six step-children. I think of them so much. We don't get to see Donna, David, and Ronnie very often because they live in Ohio. Don lives in Phoenix, Arizona. Benny and Greg live in Westmoreland, Tennessee. Benny we call "Little Benny"; he is quite a character. Just to meet him is a pure joy, and Don too; they are just crazy kids. Crazy in a good way. They are constantly pulling jokes on somebody. Roy Orbison once said to get Don and Little Benny and my Donnie and Corey together was like a three-ring circus; and believe me, it is.

Corey now lives in Hickman County. He and his girlfriend work for the stagehands' union. Everybody knows Corey; everybody likes him. He's a character. He plays a mean rock-and-roll guitar, too; Roy Orbison was here one night and Corey got wound up on his guitar, and Roy thought he was great.

———

Roy Orbison – we loved Roy. Even after twenty-five years we still miss him. He spent a lot of time with us. When he died, it was a tough time for us. He died in Benny's arms. It was really upsetting to read a magazine article I picked up about a week or two after Roy's death, where the guy who wrote it quoted somebody as saying Roy the night before his death was at Jean Shepard's house drinking and partying. What a lie! Roy had been to our house, but anybody who knows us could tell that quote was wrong. I'll put it this way: the music people, they had more parties in this town, but Benny and me never did go. We was invited to every one. But there was a lot of drinking. I don't have no time for a drunk. Never have been one to party. The guy who wrote that article was full of it. He could have learned the bittersweet story of Roy's last night if he had asked us.

Roy was one of our best friends. Since my husband worked for him for eight years, taking care of his business and everything, they became very, very close, and I in turn got to know Roy well.

Well anyway, that night he and Benny was going out to do some Christmas shopping, and afterwards we told him we hoped he would stay to dinner. He said, "Are you going to make that thingy?!" I make this salmon loaf, and it was his favorite. He never could think of the name of it; he called it "thingy." He stayed at our house a lot. He loved for me to cook for him; and I loved to do it. I never saw anyone eat like Roy. You'd make him breakfast the next morning, and he'd sit there and eat bacon and eggs and smoke a cigarette. Roy was a pretty heavy smoker.

Roy was a funny person. Just really a nice guy. He was always trying to buy us something, and Benny told him, he said, "You ain't got enough money to buy me." That night while they was shopping, Roy was trying to buy Benny a new car. Benny said, "You can't buy me a new car," and Roy come home and kept talking about it; he said, "Well let me buy Mrs. Jean one." And of course I said no.

Well anyway, after dinner that night, Roy wasn't feeling good and he said he believed he'd go to his mother's. He stayed with his mother, and they didn't live far from us at all. He thought he must be taking a cold. They had just got off the road; they'd been to Massachusetts and Ohio and all over. So he felt bad, and I gave him two Tylenol, and he went on home. And an hour later, it was all over. It was such a shock.

About an hour after he'd left, his brother called and said Roy had fell and was in the bathroom. So Benny went down to the house and went in the bathroom and picked him up. And he died in Benny's arms.

It was a horrible, horrible thing, and I hope never to go through anything like that again, especially with such a dear friend.

Roy meant the world to us. We didn't really mourn for him until about a week later when they was doing an interview on television; we broke down and had a good cry, and after that we got better. Roy was a gentleman, and one of the best friends we ever had.

Roy, we miss you and we love you.

————

Benny and I have so many great friends inside both the country industry and related music fields. We've had great friends within the ranks of our musicians. We have been tremendously blessed. I can't imagine how I would have done any of this without him. Teddy Wilburn said something when me and Benny first started going together, and we finally got married. Teddy said, "Why in the world do you think he married you?"

I said, "Well I would hope it would be because we loved one another."

Teddy just shook his head and walked away. About eight or ten years later, Teddy come up to me and said, "I need to apologize to you."

"For what?"

He said, "I didn't think it would ever work. But you all seem to be real happy."

"Well we fight like cats and dogs, you know, but who don't?"

You know, people in the business just thought that I should not remarry and be happy because of Hawkshaw Hawkins. Ernest Tubb's another one, he never was friendly toward Benny. It hurt my feelings; and it bothered Benny too. What people needed to realize was, Hawk was gone, and I had to go on living. And I certainly did – I've lived through so much with Benny.

I could not have done this without Benny. I could not have gone these past forty-five years in the business without him; and I know that, I'm not dumb. Benny gave me freedom to concentrate on my real love: singing and entertaining. And nobody could have done it better. Not only is he a fine rhythm player, but you cannot imagine all he does. You really can't. He took care of the band, he acted as manager, he went after people who needed somebody to get ripe with them when they wouldn't pay. I no longer had to think about the bus, he took care of the bus, he drove the bus – we've had seven buses and he took care of every one of them. I need to say right here that Benny is the best driver in this whole world. He has driven us probably three or four million miles over the years.

Sometimes I don't give him enough credit. Well Dad, I'm giving you your credit now, darling. I love you!!

I have a reputation as a strong person, and it is true to a great extent. When I was single, I certainly put all I had into my work and made friends along the way. When I was widowed and single again with children, I rose to that occasion. I admire anyone who is ready to withstand and find a way. But who can sincerely say they don't need someone to walk through everything with them, good times and hard times? Before I married Benny, I dealt with it. I had people looking out for me, too, producers, booking agents, and all of them were true friends. But it was better to have a partner in all these things. Benny takes care of me. I wish every woman had a husband she could rely on like him.

Me and Benny walk through it all together. Some things – you just have to find the humor in them or you'd get down. I can't even tell you how many times I've been paid for a show, and then it was a bad check. It happens to every entertainer, I could paper the walls with all of them. You travel a thousand miles to do a show, and – ! But one time we played a show for a guy who paid us a thousand dollars in five-dollar bills. After he left and we left and got back to the hotel was when we noticed: they all had the same serial number! He'd give us two hundred counterfeit five-dollar bills! The guy was long gone, there was no one there. Place was locked. We just chalked it up.

The stories of everything we've done and heard and seen could fill this whole book many times over.

————

I'd love to tell you all of Benny's and my road stories. We could talk about that a long time, and you'd just die laughing. Sometimes you laugh, sometimes you just stand in awe because these are the legends of the business. Who is left to tell you the stories I can tell, at this point in time?

Like Roy Acuff! It was always a great pleasure to work a show with Roy. I remember one time when I worked with him; this was about '69 or '70. Sonny James was on the show, and Nat Stuckey, too. Sonny opened the show and Nat followed, and then came intermission. I opened the second half of the show, and Roy would come on with his group and do the last forty-five minutes or so.

Roy was a very smart man, and I loved his show. He had a great band playing with him: Jimmy Riddle; Brother Oswald – he was one of our characters of the *Opry* – he played dobro for Acuff; there was about five or six guys, and Roy featured every one of them. That would take twenty minutes. The audience would get a little restless with it. So Roy asked me if I would mind, after he had done about ten or fifteen minutes, coming out in the middle of the show. In other words, he would start the second half and do about fifteen minutes and then bring me out. He was smart enough to see that it did break up the monotony of his show.

So we did it that way, and it worked very well. It was really fun.

It was in Buffalo, New York. While we were doing our bit, Roy stayed out there and played the snare drums – he was wonderful on them. In fact somebody took a picture of Roy on the drums with us. I wonder how many people have had the honor of having Roy Acuff as their drummer?

We worked about fifteen days like that, and it was a wonderful show. In working with Roy down through the years, especially road shows, I think by watching him I could always learn something new. He was a master of what he did, and he did it well. I truly appreciated the great contribution that this legendary person gave to the entire world. The music industry is not the same without him. I remember Roy with so much love and affection.

————

Another friend we saw a lot of on the road was "The Southern Gentleman," Sonny James. I worked with Sonny so many years ago and he was always a clean cut, good-looking young man. Half of the females in country music were in love with him. Sonny James had more consecutive number-one hit records than anybody in country music; in fact I have heard he had more than anyone, not only country. He was true to his music, and I think he totally enjoyed presenting his wonderful style of country music. For several years, Sonny has been retired. And when they put him in the Hall of Fame in 2006, it totally thrilled me to see my wonderful friend rightfully honored. He should have been in there years ago. Sonny, you and your beautiful wife, Doris, will never know how much I truly love and treasure your friendship.

Let me tell you about one time Benny and I worked with Sonny. It was in Canada. Roy Acuff was on the show, Nat Stuckey, Sonny, and myself. Back then, you had to go to the IRS and document what you earned while you were there. Benny and I walked in there to clear ourselves with the Canadian tax people, and the gentleman asked me who all was on the show. I told him Roy Acuff, Sonny James, and Snatch Nukky. I was trying to say Nat Stuckey, but for some reason or another I could not for the life of me say Nat's name. The guy looked at me real strange and I repeated "Snatch Nukky" again. I looked at Benny and said, "Tell him who I'm trying to say." With a very straight face, Benny said: "Snatch Nukky." I could have crawled under the stage. I love you Sonny, thanks for the memories.

———

Another one of the great singers in our business, Tammy Wynette, was also a good friend. I still miss her. As I will explain in the next chapter, we did have one situation. But I loved Tammy Wynette. She was a very, very sweet person. I remember one time, we was working in Alabama. This is when I was expecting Corey. She had been married for about two years to George Jones. She walked up to me; I was pretty fat in the middle, and she put her arms around me and patted my stomach and said, "That's what I want." Then a few months later, she was pregnant with Georgette. I'll never forget that. I love you, Tammy. God bless you, darling.

We also got to work a lot with Johnny Cash and June Carter Cash. Needless to say, I knew these characters for a long, long time. I can't say that June Carter was a great singer, but I enjoyed her comedy so much. She was a very, very funny lady, and I wish she was still here doing the great comedy that she did back then. When singing with her mother and sisters, she did a great job.

As far as Johnny goes, I knew and worked with him for many years. Anybody who listened to John sing knew that what was great about him as a singer was not his voice but that he was a great stylist. That is something: if somebody can create a style and keep it going year after year. John had such a distinct voice that it was certainly not hard to figure it out when he sang.

John and I worked some of the roadshows with the Opry together, and I worked with them overseas later, at the last International Festival of Country Music in London in 1991 at the Wembley Arena. People just call it the Wembley Festival. I worked it three times: in 1975, 1977, and 1991. (That was the last one. Then about a year ago they brought it back.)

Mervyn Conn, the promoter who staged the Wembley Festival, would cut off the PA after your ten or fifteen minutes were up. When he cut me off, the people were requesting songs. He wouldn't let us sing them; he didn't even give us a chance to say good night.

I was walking through the hall looking for Conn, 'cause I was going to kill him. I saw John sitting in his dressing room as I was walking by, and I told him who I was looking for and why. John said, "God don't kill him until I get to him."

———

Maybe if I had to pick just one person I have more fond memories of than any single individual we worked with, it would be Grandpa Jones. We thoroughly enjoyed that man. Thank God there will only be one Grandpa Jones!! Nobody can imitate him and nobody wants to imitate him. I speak with love in my heart for this man. And yes, his friends really called him Grandpa. Some of us called him Leather, I'm not sure why. I think it was because he said he'd spent so many hours on the road, his ass was leather.

Grandpa Jones, Bill Anderson, and myself used to film *The Bill Anderson Show*. I was the first girl singer on it. We had to go to Charlotte,

North Carolina, to do the show; so when we went, we would do four shows at a time and that would make four weeks' worth. If you made a mistake, you had to do it all over again. Every time Grandpa Jones would sing a song, I would sing one; then we would go to black. In other words, they would just stop the taping; that gave the station time to do their commercials. You would do your song, and it would go black; three more songs, and it would go to black. Since Grandpa and me took the first two turns, then if group number three messed up, we had to do ours over again. Grandpa had a terrible temper; one day I remember when I told him that we had to do our numbers over, he got real red in the face. His wife, Ramona, just told him to go and do our section again. Ramona worried about him.

So I told him one day, "If you don't settle down, you will have a heart attack." I felt real bad when Grandpa had a heart attack years later; I felt like I had caused it.

Grandpa was probably one of the funniest people that had been on the face of this earth. He had a comeback for everything.

He was building his house out in Goodlettsville, Tennessee, and was drilling for water. He must have drilled five or six wells and he would hit sulfur water. He invited me and Benny to come out to see him. He said, "But when you come by, be careful that you don't fall in a well."

He and Bill Carlisle was talking one night, and Bill found out that he had lost a beef steer. Bill told him, "Call me in the morning after church, and I will come over and help you look for that steer." As everyone knows, Grandpa was a real forgetful person. So Bill waited until two or three o'clock in the afternoon and Grandpa had not called him, so he called Grandpa.

Bill said, "You didn't call me to help you find that steer." Grandpa said, "I found him." Bill said, "You did, where?"

"In the freezer."

Grandpa built their house up on a hill.  Every winter he had trouble. It would rain and then turn to ice, so they had a hard time getting in and out. This one time it was calling for snow, and Ramona, his wife, told him, "You need to go to the grocery store and pick up some stuff before it snows. We won't be able to get out." Well he didn't go, and of course it snowed.

The next morning, there was nothing to fix for breakfast. He got to the store okay, but when he got back with the groceries, he couldn't make it up the hill in the car. So he went and got a wheelbarrow and loaded it with the groceries.  He started up the hill and, of course, the wheelbarrow turned over and all the groceries rolled back down the hill.

He loaded up about three times, and lost the groceries every time.

Finally, he got to the top of the hill with them, and he opened the back door and threw the groceries inside the door. The eggs were all broken, the milk was smashed, and everything was a mess.  He told Ramona, "Here's your damn groceries."

Nobody can know all the funny little things that Grandpa did.  You just had to be around him. One night we was in Canada, and I was happy to be there. We were looking for our hotel.  We could see its neon sign on top of the hotel, but we couldn't seem to get to it. So Grandpa stopped the car and asked this man how to get to the hotel.

The man didn't know, so Grandpa just drove on. He said the man was Otto Kruger von Haufinstein.

I said, "Why did you call him that?"

He said, "Because they are all alike and they say the same thing."

About ten or fifteen years later, I bought a schnauzer puppy and I named him Otto Kruger von Haufinstein.

Here is another story about Grandpa. He went downtown to check out buying a new car.  He was standing there looking at this car when this salesman walked up to him and said,"Are you thinking about a new car?"

Grandpa said, "No, I was thinking about sex, but I can be talked into a new car."

Ramona said he snored horrible. One time she let Vic Willis tape Grandpa snoring. So Willis brought and put that tape in his locker (Vic's and Grandpa's lockers was side by side). He left it playing; it went on for thirty minutes. Everybody was standing around laughing when Grandpa come walking up. He heard it and looked at them and he said, "Ain't that funny."

Some of my finest times in the music business have been around Grandpa Jones who I dearly loved.

———

Here's a funny memory I have of the Wilburns. Around 1968 or 1969, we were on the *Opry* with Teddy and Doyle Wilburn when they were the hosts. Back then you would do two numbers, and then go and sit on the stage somewhere. Then they would call you back to do another song. So we did our first number. After we got through with our song, Doyle came back out and said, "Well ladies and gentlemen, that winds up the *Grand Ole Opry* for tonight – come back and see us real soon."

It was only around ten. The *Opry* always ran till midnight. Doyle came off and I said, "What's happening?" He said, "We just had a bomb threat and I am getting the hell out of here."

As we rushed the hallway, Teddy says, "I am going to my dressing room first, because I am not leaving my Nudie suits here."

Thank God, there was no bomb; so he didn't get blown up.

(You probably know about "Nudie suits" – the elegant, embroidered, rhinestone western suits first made popular when Pee Wee King's band began wearing them on stage. Nudie Cohn was the name of the famous tailor and designer who custom-made them.)

One night Doyle came in, running late for the show. He went straight to his dressing room. In less than a minute, two policemen came right in after him. Come to find out, he had been drinking and he was coming down Briley Parkway on the wrong side of the road. They waited until he finished his show and they took him off to jail.

--------

The Wilburns were influential in helping Loretta Lynn make her start. They were responsible for her recording contract and they put a lot of money into her career. I know they worked diligently and were responsible for a lot of Loretta's success. Loretta owes a big debt of gratitude to the Wilburn Brothers, which was left out of her story in *Coal Miner's Daughter*. She set the record straight in her later book *Still Woman Enough*, but some people may not know that.

Loretta Lynn put in *Coal Miner's Daughter* something that I had a talk with her about. This was right after we'd just moved into the new Opry house, the early '70s. A friend of mine came up to me and said, "Jean what do you mean trying to keep Loretta from joining the Opry?" I said I never did no such thing. My friend showed me the book, where Loretta says when she came to Nashville, the women of the *Grand Ole Opry* had a meeting to try to keep her off of the *Grand Ole Opry*. She wrote that Kitty Wells was not involved in the meeting. Well, there weren't a lot of women at that time, so that left who? Me and Goldie Hill and I don't know who else.

I confronted Loretta with this one night backstage. She said, "Well people told me that."

I told her, "Loretta, don't believe everything people say. You are writing hearsay, but that was totally, totally false." I said maybe my feelings should be hurt that I wasn't invited to the meeting!

I knew of no meeting to try to keep Loretta Lynn off the *Grand Ole Opry*. At the time, I didn't know a thing about Loretta so I wouldn't have had no reason to try and keep her off. It was her career. Go for it.

Loretta and I are good friends. Her career has been great and she has been a great credit to country music for over fifty years. She joined the Opry in 1962. She came from very humble beginnings and worked hard for her place in country music.

————

As you know, many of the artists I worked with throughout these past sixty years I met in California. One of these was Little Jimmy Dickens. When I was just getting into the business, I had the pleasure of working on a show with him one night. At that time, he had a steel guitar player by the name of Walter Haynes. I fell in love with Walter, who looked exactly like Tony Curtis and was such a great musician. He later played on a lot of my records I cut in Nashville.

To a lot of us, Jim is known by his nickname, Tater. I think Hank Williams gave him that name, I'm not sure.

Well let me tell you a classic. Tater had a drinking problem – let me say this tongue in cheek, and with a lot of love in my heart. One night (this was after I married Benny) they had a huge *Grand Ole Opry* show in Maryland. It was in a big arena and they probably had twenty Opry acts. Everybody was there: Minnie Pearl, Jim & Jesse, Bill Anderson, along with Jimmy Dickens. There were so many acts that everybody only did two songs. This was the first time I ever saw big television screens around.

Well little Tater could be a pain in the ass when he wanted to be. On a night when he was drinking, he was apt to be a royal pain. This was one of those nights. I was wearing kind of a low-cut dress. Back forty years ago, I was built pretty good – you know, as the saying goes, like a brick outhouse. Anyway, Tater would run up to me and his nose would come right into my chest. I would say, "Jimmy, go away, leave me alone." He like to have run me crazy. Well I went to Benny and said, "Honey, tell Tater to back off."

Tater was drunk so he didn't know what he was doing. He just kept on and on. I went out to the bus just to get away from him. When I come back in, he met me at the door. He just went on and on. I went to the ladies' room and stayed in there for thirty minutes. I'd come out and he would be there, standing and waiting for me.

I finally told Benny, "If Dickens don't leave me alone, there is going to be trouble." Finally Benny went to Jimmy and said, "Tater, you are really getting on Jean's nerves. Now she has asked you several times to back off and leave her alone. You better back off because if you don't, she's going to hurt you. If she don't hurt you, I'm going to have to."

He paid no attention to Benny. There was a cop nearby, a security guard, who knew Jimmy. He was an ex-musician or something, years ago.

Finally he went up to Jimmy and said, "Jim, now I'm your friend, but I have to tell you, if you don't leave Jean alone, we are going to have some problems here. For the last two or three hours, you have just run her crazy. So I'm asking you as a friend to back off and let this go. If Jean decides to, we'll have to take you outside."

He settled down after that. But, boy, you talk about a royal pain in the ass when he was drinking, was little Jimmy Dickens. But I love you Jim.

# CHAPTER NINE

# "SLIPPIN' AWAY"

Like I said, I think probably one of the biggest mistakes I made in my career was leaving Capitol. I went to United Artists and had a couple hits with them. But it wasn't the recording company that Capitol was. It was a sad day when I left Capitol.

At the time, I thought I was being lost in the shuffle and that a change would do me good. But in the long run, it didn't do me that much good. When I called Ken Nelson and asked for a release, it was a very touching time. Ken said he had to go before the board of directors to get a release. He said he would call me in a couple of weeks.

After two weeks, I called and asked him, "Did you talk to them yet?" He said, "I didn't have the heart to bring it up to them. But I will."

About the third time I called him, he said, "Jean, are you sure this is what you want to do?"

I said, "Yes, I am."

"I promise you, next week I will talk to them about it," he replied.

When I called him back, he asked me again if I was sure. He got real choked up. Then when he started to cry I started to cry. After almost twenty-two years, I was leaving him.

He said, "If you are sure this is what you want, you can have your release."

Now that I look back, it was a dumb thing to do. But I let Larry Butler talk me into leaving Capitol. United Artists enticed me with a pretty big check to sign with them. Larry had been at Capitol and moved to United (I actually got him that job). He was my producer on *Seven Lonely Days*.

I stayed with United for about five or six years. For a year or two it was pretty good. My A&R man there, Kelso Herston, we began to have friction. For one thing I didn't like him coming in my sessions drinking. 'Cause that was my money we was messing with. And eventually I had a disagreement with the president of United Artists, too; because he told me a lie. I'll leave it at that.

My single "Slippin' Away" hit number four on the charts after I signed with United, but my association with them was in general a disappointment. Maybe United was partially to blame, but not entirely so. The times we were living in played a part.

Throughout the '70s, the country music industry was hard hit. There was so much going on; not only in music but in the world. It was an unstable era.

For one thing, anyone over the age of fifty can remember the anxiety at that time about Vietnam. Like most Americans, I felt a love for the soldier and appreciated their sacrifice. And I also saw it was an outrage how they were being sent into Vietnam for motives that many of us could see were a mess. The soldiers were paying the price. I often heard from fans who were in the service.

I remember a young man who walked up to me after a show in Denver, Colorado. He was in the Air Force. He started talking and told me he was being shipped to Vietnam. I asked him if he knew what we were doing over there. He said that "we were doing it for our country." It broke my heart.

Some time after US forces left Vietnam, I was working in Pennsylvania. This boy in an Army uniform came up to me after the show. He asked me if I was Jean Shepard. He said his best buddy over there, who would take my picture out of his pack and kiss it every morning and night, used to be a big fan of mine. I said, "He *used to* be?" The boy said, "He didn't make it back."

And I had close friends whose boys were over there, too. My friend Jan Howard was tragically affected by that war. She had two sons serving there. David was killed; his brother Corky escorted him home. When I heard the news I remember I was driving to California to visit my dad, who was recovering from a heart attack (Daddy survived another couple of years). I called Jan (I had one of the first mobile phones in this town), but all I could say was I was thinking of her. What is there to say?

I have thought about this next story so many times. This boy had just returned from Vietnam. He had gotten discharged in New York City, and was hailing a cab. The cabbie asked him, "Are you just getting back?" And asked where was he coming from. When the soldier said Vietnam, the cabbie spit in his face.

I realize WWII was a devastating thing; we lost so many young men. But Vietnam vets did not get their share of glory for what they'd done. After I'd heard several stories of this nature, I developed a sympathy toward these vets. So, ten or twelve years later when Vic Willis asked me to help with the *Vietnam Vets Show* I was glad to do that. We held about three shows, and the proceeds were donated to Vietnam Vets through their base camp in Hendersonville. But the *Opry* stopped donating their space; they started charging five or six thousand; and that put an end to it.

Another conflict we were up against in the '70s was, the record companies were making it hard to keep country music purely country. It started when the Beatles became popular here.

Thank God I had had a record printed just before the Beatles came out. I didn't get another record for a year. All the pressing plants were busy pressing out Beatles records. The Beatles were with Capitol. My Mother, I realized how wise she was when I heard her make this observation; she said, "This country was just fine until the Beatles got off that airplane with that long hair."

The whole country music industry hinged on what the Beatles did. But while the radio was playing Beatles music, we were still out playing on the road, and the fans were still there. They wanted to hear us. They were waiting for us to come back.

It's funny though; while the Beatles were over here dominating our charts, country artists were popular over there. Jim Reeves had "I Love You Because" in the British Top 10 for several weeks running, challenging the Beatles. He often kept number-one songs on the UK's charts.

Still, the country artists felt there had to be some way to take a stand for traditional music here.

————

Let me touch briefly on an organization that was known as ACE (the Association of Country Entertainers). People said I was president of it; I wasn't ever president. But it all got dumped on my shoulders. And the bank took my house and everything in the end.

In 1974 I got pulled into this organization. I was on the road and had plenty else to think about. I came home one day from a show, and my housekeeper asked if I had heard of this organization: George Jones, Tammy, Conway, George Morgan, Porter – all these country artists were in it. I said no, and I kept working; I didn't pay no attention.

But it was the year Olivia Newton-John had been voted Female Singer of the Year by the CMA, and some of the traditional artists were mad. I didn't care. I was busy with my own career, and I never tried to stop anybody else's. But ACE had a couple of meetings. Someone said that Conway Twitty called some of the other ACE people and said, "We need to get Jean Shepard in on this, because she is a staunch believer in traditional country music and she stands up for what she believes in."

George Morgan was in on it, Hank Snow was in on it, and a whole bunch of people. A couple of weeks later, they called me and asked if I would serve on the board. I thought, Well that might be a good organization. The songwriters have an organization; the booking agents have an organization; the musicians have an organization. So I thought it was great that the entertainers wanted to have an organization; it would be a way for the artists to have the final word.

After they recruited me I went to two or three meetings. You had to pay a hundred dollars to belong, and they thought they'd have a meeting once a month. Some said the camaraderie would hold the country music industry together, maybe have an impact on DJs; they were controlled by the music labels.

ACE thought we needed to borrow money for an office. We went to Commerce Union Bank. The head of the bank was a gentleman named Clarence Reynolds, who was a good friend of ours. At first the group borrowed eighty thousand, I think (it has been forty years ago). All of these artists would go out and work shows, they said, and would pay off the bank.

Well folks, it never happened. I went out and worked some shows; Grandpa Jones worked some; Del Wood did. We paid down some interest. The others was supposed to go out and work some shows too. No one ever did. No one wanted to pay off the loans.

No one wanted to run the office, either. They just let the office sit there.

A girl was brought in to work in the office. Then what do you think? She ended up absconding with some of the funds. Here we go again! We had to go back to the bank and borrow another sixty or seventy thousand; but this time, they needed collateral. We lived in Gallatin, Tennessee, in a two hundred fifty–thousand dollar home. We, me and Benny, put our home up as collateral on this loan. It was very dumb of me, so everyone can call me a dumbass, because that is what I was. It was a very nice home.

I went down a couple times a week and answered mail and phone calls, or whatever. But I just didn't have the time to do that. One day I went down to the office and realized: We have got to close this down. So I started making phone calls.

I got Tammy on the phone and said, "Tammy, we are going to close this office down. I don't know how to run an office and don't have the time to run this office."

Well she just practically started crying. She said, "Oh Jean, please don't close the office down, don't close ACE down. Please don't do it. We will do some shows to take up the slack. That organization was born in George's and my home."

So I said, "Well Tammy, why haven't you paid your dues for the last two years?" That was the end of that conversation.

We got a call one day from the bank, "What are we going to do about this loan?" So we went down to talk to this one man. He said, "Have you all thought about filing bankruptcy?"

Benny looked at him and said, "Not until right now we haven't."

So because my so-called good friends in ACE never did work a show, or ever tried to pay that money back, guess who was on the losing end? I was. Not one of them ever came forward and said, I'll help; nor, I'm sorry. Vic Willis was going to; I think he had put his house up, too; but his house was in his wife's name so the bank couldn't touch it.

(Let me say this: Vic Willis was probably one of the best friends I ever had. We both came from Oklahoma, and I had seen him lose his two brothers. I lived through that with him; I held his hand and helped him. When he got killed in a freak car accident in 1995, it broke my heart.)

I think it was probably was around 1976 or 1977 when all this happened. Through a lot of trials and tribulations, we lost everything and had to file bankruptcy. We just decided that we would do the best we could, and that's what we've done.

There were people who didn't speak to me for fifteen years after the organization fell through. Why? I think a guilty conscience.

But let me say this, I don't hold no grudges or hard feelings against them. If they don't know what they done to me, they will know now. If you can live with it, I can live without it. The Lord has blessed us and we have done great, so more power to those people who let me down.

There were many difficulties to overcome as we climbed back out of bankruptcy. But I can tell you, the Lord provides. My husband has a lot of resourcefulness. Here we were without a bus, bankrupt, and needing now more than ever to continue touring. Benny went down to a used car lot in Gallatin, and he talked to the man there, who knew him. And just on goodwill he was able to say, If you'll let me have a car I'll pay you in six months. So we hit the road in that little Toyota sedan and made a comeback.

Putting aside the whole ACE story, throughout the '70s I did whatever I could to take a strong stand for traditional country music. Traditional artists like myself, Jimmy Dickens, Carl Smith, Hank Snow, and Ernest Tubb could see that it was getting away from us. I would get onstage and make announcements about the way country music was headed. We would get a lot of complaints that the radio stations weren't playing our records. I told people, the fans, If you want to hear my records on the radio, you have to request them. If you don't hear our records playing, you are going to have to call the disk jockey and request them. If they refuse to play them, then you can tell them that you won't buy from their sponsors.

Larry Butler called Benny and told him that I needed to quit making these announcements or United was probably going to drop me. Benny said, "I can't tell Jean to stop talking about what she believes in."

After all these years, I'm still a member of the Grand Ole Opry – for fifty-eight years. So I think my career speaks for itself. I don't know if it's my talent or they are afraid to fire me, or something. I am very grateful to the country music industry and most of all the country music fans. They have been loyal and faithful down through the years. I have enjoyed my fifty-eight years at the *Grand Ole Opry* and I hope that I have contributed something to keep it alive.

I have had a good run in country music and I wouldn't change one thing. So I guess I will just keep on trucking.

————

While the record companies were interfering with country music in the US, the market overseas was another story. In Europe they were wild about traditional country music. We did a lot of tours over there. I love going overseas.

Wembley was the first time I toured overseas. I went because the BBC asked their listeners who they would like to see at the festival and I come in number one. Right behind me was Tammy Wynette. The English people love good country music. It's wonderful to go and have ten thousand people screaming your name.

The loyalty those fans showed was so inspiring. They made me feel so popular, I could run for political office in England and win. I could be their prime minister or whatever, like Margaret Thatcher was. There was places like England, Ireland, Scotland, Germany, Austria, Sweden; I went everywhere. It is such a pleasure to go over there; they have such an appreciation for traditional country music.

In fact, I got an offer about four years ago to go to Sweden. But it is just not worth it, even if it is a good paying day. But to play for only one day, the trip would turn into four or five days. It is just not worth it.

But we fought an uphill battle here for several years, going against the tide of what the corporate people wanted. And although we put in a lot of muscle to stand up for it, what has always saved country music was the music itself. It is a strong, distinctive style and the fans remained loyal to it. Country music songs are written for an old boy that's been out working ten hours a day, and it just tells the story of his life. It's music for the working man. Country music tells a story. It tells it in a plain, very direct way.

The corporate people, to them a good song comes from their market research. To the fan, a good song is the kind that comes about from real life. A writer gets an idea; maybe his girlfriend will say something to him and he'll think, That's a title for a good song. And it grows from there. Country music speaks to the soul of a country music fan. They can relate to everything that guy has wrote in that song.

The music survives because the fans love it. A good song goes to their heart. It's something a guy can listen to and say, "I like that." Something you can relate to. Then it's a hit song. Or used to be. Not some "I fell in love with my tractor" something!

I don't know if I could pick one song that's my favorite of all those I've recorded. I liked most of the songs I recorded; about ninety percent. But then you'd have a silly song like "Franklin County Moonshine." I did not want to do that one, Ken Nelson thought I should! I had some great ballads that people didn't get to hear; the disk jockeys don't play them at all.

But as an artist, sometimes you live those songs. They become special to you. There's always a little part of each song that will touch you. Like "Two Little Boys." I still get a lot of requests for that. Maybe one song I could say I liked best was "Think I'll Go Somewhere and Cry Myself to Sleep." I've been there. I've done that. I've cried myself to sleep a lot of times.

Sometimes a song will just fit you. You feel it in your heart, feel it in your bones. If you record a song and you really like it, you'll put everything you got in it. "Another Neon Light," that's a well-written song; it's a song with a lot of truth in it. I love a song that's well-written and put together. I like "The Tennessee Waltz." That's a well-written song. And it became the state song. That's the one, ha! Pee Wee King and Redd Stewart wrote it while they were driving home from Kentucky, between Bowling Green and Nashville.

———————

Pee Wee King and Redd Stewart – these guys were two of my favorite people. They wrote some of the greatest songs ever. Besides "The Tennessee Waltz," of course, Redd wrote a big pop song called "You Belong to Me," which was recorded by Jo Stafford. I truly loved these gentlemen.

Their contributions to our industry have been above and beyond the call of duty. Pee Wee was put in the Hall of Fame in 1974, but they didn't put Redd in with him. What a shame! Redd belongs there. Shame on you, Country Music Hall of Fame.

Good songwriters can write anything. Pee Wee would say that he helped Redd write, but I don't know if Pee Wee was that smart! (Saying this tongue-in-cheek.) He played the accordion, but of the two, Redd was the musician and Pee Wee was more the business mind.

A few years back, I was on the phone with Pee Wee checking on him after he had his stroke. This was in the '90s. I always called him Wee Pee, so I said, "Wee Pee, how are you doing?"

He said, "Pretty good, sweetheart, but my left hand is not too good. But of course my left hand never was any good." He was always a lot of fun, even up till our last conversations. He was a great talent, and also a friend. I continued to call and check on him, even after he was no longer able to speak; his family would tell me how he was.

The right song, even if you've been in the profession a long time, it can move you to tears. Every artist has even had a moment when performing a song, and – you just can't. Sometimes you cry. I was at Sandstone, Minnesota, not too long ago, maybe two years. I started to do, "If I Could Hear My Mother Pray Again." Well I just couldn't get through it. The audience? They just got real quiet. They let me set there a minute, they let me have my moment. I knew all those musicians, and they were right there with me. I think Benny was surprised.

––––––

As I said, my hit record "Slippin' Away" was with United. The first three or four years I had real good success with them. But they just could not keep the wheel rolling. Every time I turned around, I had to deal with someone else. I had three different producers. I had some good success with Larry Butler. But he began having troubles of his own, so I hooked up with George Richey, who was Tammy Wynette's husband.

I truly didn't think he was interested in my career. He had become Tammy's manager – and rightly so, but he was interested in her career more than mine. We didn't have any harsh words over my career and I didn't expect to.

"Slippin' Away" was written by one of my favorite songwriters, Bill Anderson. It was my biggest hit in about ten or fifteen years. He could write a song that just kind of fit me. He is still writing; it tickles me to see – these new writers will be coming out with their hits, then Bill will just creep in with a good one. He slides right in and gets one. There's no stopping Bill Anderson.

I first met Bill in the mid '50s when he was a DJ. Bill and I laugh about this. It was down in Georgia. Hawkshaw was on the show, Ernest Tubb, and gosh, somebody else; there was three or four acts on the show. So he was interviewing me, and after a while he just kept talking and talking until I thought, Why is he talking so much? I saw he was running out of things to say. So finally it dawned on me, this young man had never done an interview before. He didn't know how to get out of it. Finally I said, "Bill, I need to let you go and talk to some of the other artists on the show." I later learned, I was the first artist he had ever interviewed.

Bill Anderson is a good friend of mine. And let me tell you, Bill Anderson, as far as I am concerned, is the consummate entertainer. He knows just exactly what to say and when to say it to the crowd. To be introduced by Bill Anderson – he's the best I have ever seen. He works a crowd.

I'll tell you another memory during my United Artists days, but a bittersweet memory. You know I'd known George Morgan many years. George was a person that I just loved with all my heart. Not only did he have one of the smoothest voices in country music, he had the greatest sense of humor that I have ever seen.

He loved playing tricks. They had this guy who played fiddle, Don Slayman. Some of the musicians made up this tale where they were going to convince Don that George was so depressed it was worrying them. This was all a practical joke. They kept it up for about three or four weeks. Then finally, the way I heard it, one day when they were at a hotel, these musicians took Don out somewhere, and while they were gone, George bought a bottle of iodine. They came back to the hotel and went to George's room. When George heard them coming, he ran the tub full of water and poured in some iodine. When they came in, George slid down under the water. They opened the bathroom door and saw George; Don thought he had gone and killed himself. Don almost had a heart attack. They did carry it a little bit too far. So not only do we remember George Morgan as a great singer, but someone who would do anything for a laugh.

But one day in 1975, I was in the recording studio. We was just starting the session when the phone rang. My producer answered it. He took a couple of minutes, and then came out of the control room.

He put his arms around me and said, "Why don't you give us some keys and we will lay down some tracks."

I knew that George Morgan had just died. I think I had a premonition. I knew that the call was about George Morgan. I just totally lost it. It just broke my heart. Weldon Myrick and a lot of these musicians were there; Leon Rhodes, Jimmy Capps; we all just broke down and cried.

They said, "Why don't we all go home and do this next week."

So George Morgan, I say to you, "You stopped my world that day."

# CHAPTER TEN

# BACKSTAGE DRAMA

Back then, as you worked with your fellow artists and the musicians, you formed friendships, and your friendships were lasting. You shared things with other artists that you didn't share with another person; we were all on the same flow. It's a shame country music has changed so much.

Country music as I have lived it has always been a family. We work and eat and travel together, we check on each other when someone's sick. We commiserate. On the other hand, we even get irritated, like people do who become close. Then we try to iron things out, as you've seen. We play and we relax together, too. And we watch each other's kids. I used to go with Jan Howard to her sons' ballgames. Another young man I've talked a little about, Hank Jr., grew up on the road with us.

At this point, from the time he was a teenager until his early twenties, everyone knows he and his mother, Audrey, were always on the outs. I was always trying to convince him she loved him. She worshipped him, just worshipped that child.

This one time when he was sixteen or seventeen we was leaving town. (I rode on the bus a lot with them, did a lot of shows with them.) This was Thanksgiving night. We'd all eaten Thanksgiving dinner and we was going to Charleston, South Carolina. They couldn't find Hank nowhere.

We was leaving at twelve. About twelve-thirty he come into the house and got to fussing with his mother. He was not a pleasant child at this time in his life to be around. I said, "I'm going on out to the bus."

Well Junior walked out behind me and plopped down in one of the seats right there by me. I thought, Oh no.

That next morning as we was riding along, Audrey said we were going to stop and eat. She walked up through the bus and she said to him, "Honey, do you want to eat?"

And he said, "Audrey, you son of a bitch, get outta my face!"

I'd never heard that, just could not believe he said that to his mother. Before I knew it I just popped him right in the mouth. I said, "Don't you talk to your mother like that!" I thought, "Oh God, he's going to hit me."

When we got to wherever we was going, we didn't check in; we went straight to the venue, planning to do our show and leave. I went and sat on a park bench backstage. Here come Junior and he laid his head in my lap and stretched out like he was going to sleep. I kinda bounced his head with my knee, and I said, "Hank Jr., you should be ashamed of yourself."

He said, "Oh hell she bothers me all the time." She tried to force him to walk in his daddy's shoes and he wasn't ready for them. She just wanted him to be a star. And she made him a star.

He started to call her names again, and I said, "Hush. Don't repeat it. I don't want to hear it. Hank Jr., that's your mother. You better stop and think about what you're doing." I just really ragged him out.

She come upstairs a little while later (the dressing rooms was downstairs). She said, "Junior, do you want me to fix your hair?" She'd comb and fix his hair every night. He said, "Oh. Hell yes, Audrey. Come on."

She came up to me later – it was pitiful, it just broke my heart; she said, "Did you say something to Junior?"

I said, "Why?"

She said, "He was almost nice to me."

Almost nice? I was ashamed. Later I said to him again, "That's your mother, she loves you."

He said, "I wish to hell you was my mother."

I said, "I'd have killed you if you'd been born to me." He always called me Mama after that.

———

I reminded him of all those times a couple years ago at the Ryman; he didn't remember it. He said, "I want you to tell my kids that."

I said, "You tell your kids what an asshole you was." (You can't see me when I'm telling this, so you don't know how it is said with a smile. Junior and I are on very good terms.)

In August 1975 when Hank Jr. fell off that mountain in Montana, Audrey went to the hospital and stayed with him several weeks. She was the first to get to him, from what I understand, when they took him to the hospital. I think he was out there something like two months before they brought him home. He had half the mountain in his face.

She was not a well woman, either. Audrey didn't even live out that year. By November, she was gone. She died at her home, one day before the government would have taken it (the IRS had been in the process of taking everything she owned).

He called me the day after she died. It was going to be a private funeral. He said, "Mama you come to the funeral if you want to, we'd love to have you."

I said, "No, it's your time to grieve; you do it your own way."

When he was in his late twenties, a year or so after his mother had died, we worked a show at the University of Wisconsin. We worked a lot of shows with Hank Jr. He wanted to come in and listen to me sing. He said, "You're still the best damn country girl singer."

Even that long after his accident, there was still further surgery and healing to do. He still had this bad eye. He said, "Mama, you want to see my face?"

I said, "No, not if you don't to want show it to me."

"No, I want you to see it."

He pulled me over in this little exit like, lifted those sunglasses, I saw the way it was, and I patted him on the cheek. "That don't look bad, son."

"You just say that 'cause you love me."

I said, "I do love you."

He got real quiet for a minute, said, "I know another mother who loved me too." That's the closest he'd ever come to admitting his feelings for her.

Audrey was a good person; she meant well. She let people use her. This one night, I remember she called me about ten o'clock. She said, "What you doing, sweetheart?"

I said, "Sitting here with the kids."

She wanted me to come to San Juan, Puerto Rico. She had a whole bunch of people, she flew them down and they were partying.

I said, "Audrey, I can't come down there; I got two kids. Anyway you travel with a different crowd than I do."

She said, "Aw, I'll send them all home and you come."

She smelled so good; she wore Arpege cologne. One time I said, "Audrey you smell so good, you got the best smelling cologne." Two, three weeks later we got on the bus. She had a great big bottle of it. It must have been a quart. She said, "This is for you."

People would talk about her, "She ain't nothing but a —", this and that, and I'd say, "Well don't hang around her and use her money." People didn't like me when I was around her. I just really liked her. She was good to me, and I hope I was good to her.

———

This is like any other community, you might rub some people the wrong way from time to time. And then you have to decide whether it's worth it to be mad or have somebody mad at you. In any community, someone will get crossways with you for no reason. But you can keep on being good to them. Then the story can have a different ending. I'm thinking of two good examples. First let me talk a little about Bill Monroe.

I have always truly loved traditional country music; even though I am an artist, I am also a fan. I have to say one of my greatest loves is bluegrass music. I worked with Bill and so many others all over the country. I worked with him at Bean Blossom and the *Grand Ole Opry* so many times.

When I first met Bill, it seemed that he was so standoffish, as a lot of the bluegrass musicians could come across. But I know this, you have got to make a move towards showing these people that you really like them. I think that's because bluegrass musicians took a back seat for so many years, and few people really ever appreciated the music. In the last twenty-five to thirty years, bluegrass music has made great strides in the industry.

Over the last twenty-five years or so, I had really gotten close to Bill Monroe. A little story comes to mind about him.

Somebody sent me a tape of a song that had a tongue-in-cheek title – it was called "I Don't Wanna Cabin in the Valley, I Just Wanna Shack Up in the Hills." Well I thought that this was a funny little song.

I went to Roy Acuff and said, "I got a hit song for you." He thought it was one of the funniest he had heard.

I told several of the stars – Bill Carlisle, George Morgan – and they all thought the song was hilarious.

I went into the dressing room and told Bill, "I've got a hit song somebody sent me. It's called, 'I Don't Wanna Cabin in the Valley, I Just Wanna Shack Up in the Hills'."

Well Bill Monroe got mad at me; he was furious. He said, "You're making fun of people born in cabins."

I said, "No, no."

He said, "I was born and raised in a cabin and you are making fun of people living in cabins." He didn't catch it.

I said, "No, it's a joke."

He never did catch it. Tater Tate, one of his guys, told him it was a joke but he still wasn't happy about it. He quit speaking to me.

About six or eight months later, he went into the hospital for open-heart surgery. Well anyhow, I sent him a little artificial plant with a note on it. I wrote, "I don't care if you are mad at me, you old fart, I still love you." Well they said he got quite a kick out of it.

Then a couple months later when he came back to the *Opry*, he came down the hall and he said, "Howdy, howdy." If he said that twice, you were really in good with him, but if he only said it once, you were borderline. I said to Benny, "Well I'm back in Bill's good graces."

Needless to say, Bill Monroe will be sorely missed in our industry. He was a man who loved and believed in his music. So I say not only the music industry lost a great friend when Bill died in 1996, so did I.

———

It was along about the same time as my Hank Jr. story when I had a to-do with Hank Snow over sharing a dressing room at the *Opry*. I shared a dressing room with Hank for about twelve years. He was a senior member at the time, so he could swing his weight. Benny had asked him if we could use it, he said yes. But then he changed his mind; he didn't want us in his dressing room.

Benny asked him one night if we could come in and rehearse. So we did. About a week later, Hal Durham, the manager, called me and said that Hank had called him and said that I was bothering him in the dressing room.

The next week I told Hank, "I don't see your damn name on this damn dressing-room door and you are not big enough to throw me out."

I was determined that I was not going to be pushed out of this dressing room. We always paid him the respect that he deserved. I made all my guests leave when he came in. He had a picture of himself and Ernest Tubb on the wall. Benny asked him if it would be okay to have a picture of me in here too, and he said yes. So Benny put up the picture, and Hank got mad because the picture was bigger than his. At this time, I have to say that I didn't realize that Hank was in the beginning stages of dementia. The only thing I know is that I wanted to get along with him.

We finally quit using the dressing room. He called Ruth Bauer, a friend of mine, and said he wanted her to get the picture of me out of the dressing room.

He told Ruth, "I don't know why Jean and Benny aren't coming around any more." And she said, "You ran them off."

I came in to get the picture one night and I said to him, "You want that picture down we'll take it down." I was taking it down and I told him, "Hank, you are a cantankerous old jackass."

He looked up at me and said, "Thank you, Jean."

I told him he could take the dressing room and shove it.

This really hurt me and this feud went on for about six to eight months. I felt so bad because I really and truly loved this man. He was an icon in the business.

So one night we were passing the dressing-room door, and he was sitting in there in one of the chairs. I thought, I have to make my peace with this man.

I went in and walked up to him and said, "Hank, I am really sorry that things went as far as they did. I am not sorry for what I said, because you are a pompous little ass, but I want you to know one thing, above everything else in this world. I truly love you."

He reached up with his hand and touched my cheek and he had tears in his eyes; he said, "We can fix it, can't we Jean?" And he said, "I love you too."

Let me tell you a sad story about Hank Snow. This one night, we sat in the dressing room and talked about him being an abused child. He told me this story.

He said the winter when he was about nine or ten years old, in Nova Scotia, Canada, his daddy beat the hell out of him and threw both him and his baby sister, who was six or seven years old, out in the snow. He carried his sister on his back to the neighbor's house, which was about three or four miles.

Now through the years, Hank Snow was probably capable of acting like a jerk, but about forty years ago he told me he had become a Christian; so then he made up his mind to try to make things right with his dad.

He said, "I thought that I should try and find my dad to tell him that I forgave him for all the abuse."

He searched for about a year; he finally found his dad in a nursing home. Hank said he walked in and his dad was sitting in a wheelchair. They talked for a little while. Then Hank told him, "Dad, the reason I came by was I wanted to tell you that I forgive you for all the abuse."

He said that old man jumped out of that wheelchair – he was a big man – and just shook his fists and said, "I don't want your goddamn forgiveness."

When he told me this, it got me really upset; it hurt me so bad.

I told him, "Remember, Hank, what you did was what the Lord wanted you to do. You told your dad you forgave him and that's all you can do." I could tell this really hurt him.

I could not believe he was telling me all this, because Hank just didn't talk to people a lot. We'd had some hard times over his dressing room but in the meantime we'd become good friends.

In 1999 when Hank passed away, I was asked by his son, Jimmie, to speak at his funeral. It was one of the hardest things I have ever done. I told them how much I thought of Hank, and the stories about the dressing room.

In the eulogy I said, "I know when I die and go to heaven, Hank Snow is going to be standing there saying, 'Jean, you can't come in this dressing room,' but I am going to say, 'I am here Hank, I love you, and I am going to stay, so you take it up with the Lord'."

———

It is not just the good times that make true friends. We've seen our friends through it all: laughter and tears.

In December of 1982, we had to go over to Knoxville to pick up a bus for the Osborne Brothers.  Benny has always been a good judge as to what was good and what was bad in buses, so he has several times helped friends buy a bus.  We were on the way back with the bus. I turned the radio on, and every song they played was Marty Robbins songs. I knew that Marty was gone.  He had had a heart attack about a week before. I had lost another great friend, one I loved and admired very much.

———

When you see how many of our stories come back to the subject of buses, you'll know we have been on the road about half our lives. There's another legendary country friend of ours, I've got a strange bus story on him. It's Merle Travis. We were friends for many years. I don't know too many stories about him, just one real good bus story and one odd little memory, one of those things that sticks in your mind. It was one time when he wanted some chewing gum. I had just put a piece of chewing gum in my mouth and he said, "Give me some gum."  I said, "I ain't got any, Trav." He said, "Well give me what you've got in your mouth." So I opened my mouth, and he just reached in and took my gum.

But back to the bus story. We had this one bus, and this was just the weirdest thing in the world. We would have little things happen to it. We'd have a flat tire, or the starter would go out or something.  We would be sitting on the side of the road, and within an hour or so, here would come Merle Travis. This happened a half dozen times. After about the third time, I told Benny, "This is so weird; every time something happens, Travis comes along."

One time we was in Mississippi going down to New Orleans, and the bus broke down. We sat there for six hours, and I said, "Travis, where the hell are you?"  He didn't come by that day.

But I loved Merle Travis. He was such a great talent. I know that when Hank Thompson would record in California, Travis would pick guitar on Hank's records. Hank would go home with Travis and try to learn what Travis had picked on the record.

I told him, "Hank, give it up, you ain't going to be a Merle Travis."

I truly did love him. Oh Lord, to have known these people; to talk about them is a total joy to me.

———

Benny and Charlie Louvin kept a running practical joke about their buses. I'll tell you about Charlie.

What a singer. You know, of course, the Louvin Brothers' music. There are only a handful of brother duets; and the Louvin Brothers, as far as I am concerned, rank at the top. The harmony that the Louvin Brothers created has never been duplicated. Charlie sang great. But when Ira added the tenor part, it just made the sound that was wonderful to everybody's ears. I worked with Charlie and Ira quite a bit down through the years. Charlie was the one that I think helped hold the duet together. Ira had a drinking problem and could be one of the most obnoxious human beings that God put on this earth. I think that Ira had just so many problems that he didn't know how to deal with them.

After Ira died in a car accident in '65, I was glad that Charlie kept singing; because as I have said before he was one of the most underrated country music singers.

In 2001 they finally inducted the Louvin Brothers into the Hall of Fame. Even to literally his last days, Charlie was still very much into the music industry and still working. When he would go onstage, I always loved to go and listen to him sing. Charlie would not have anyone sing with him that was not the best. Singing with Charlie, you had to be the best. So when I hear Charlie sing, I have to just salute him and say in my heart, "Attaboy, Charlie."

———

Here's a little story. Back some years ago, me and Benny had a ten-day trip coming up and our bus had to be worked on. It wouldn't be ready in time for us to leave. Well Benny and Charlie were talking and when Charlie heard that we didn't have a bus he said, "You can take my bus if you want to. I'm not busy for a while, so take it."

Benny said he wanted to lease the bus from him, and Charlie wouldn't hear of that. He said to take his bus and use it. Friends, that little gesture will tell you what a kind person Charlie was.

To show you the real Charlie Louvin: not only would he lend a friend his bus, but he had a evil side too. We would park our bus at Higgins' Gas Station in Hendersonville, along with Lester Flatt, Charlie Louvin – a bunch of us would do that. This one day, we went up to Higgins' and Charlie was sitting there. He was just fixing to leave and go on the road. Well the motor on his bus was running wide open.

Charlie said, "I don't know what's the matter with it. But the gas pedal goes all the way to the floor and I have to reach down and pull it up."

Benny answered, "Well Charlie, I think I know what's wrong with it. There's a spring that releases the pedal that goes back and forth."

So Benny goes back there and shows Charlie where the spring was broken.

"You can stop out at Key Truck Stop out on Dickerson Road, they have a whole rack of them," Benny said.

"Okay I'll do that," Charlie said.

Well we went home, and a few days later we were fixing to leave and go on the road. We went down there. Benny cranked up the bus. Well that motor was running wide open.

Benny said, "Oh my gosh."

He went back and looked, and the spring was gone off of our bus. We knew that Charlie had took it. So two or three months later, we was going out of town and we saw Charlie's bus coming into town. His son Sonny was driving. Benny looked in the rear-view mirror. He got Sonny on the CB and said, "Sonny, you don't have any lights on the back of the bus at all."

Sonny said, "You're kidding?"

Benny said, "No, no clearance lights, nothing."

"I'll have to get them fixed," Sonny said.

Anyway, a week or so later, we had come back in and was fixing to leave again.

Well we cranked up and got out on Interstate 65 about twenty, thirty miles, and some truck driver said, "Hey, how about that Jean Shepard bus?"

Benny said, "Hey, what about the Jean Shepard bus?"

The driver said, "I want to tell you something, you ain't got one light on the back of your bus."

Benny said, "Oh God, Louvin strikes again."

He suspected it. So he got a ladder out, because he had to get way up on the back of the bus. He said, "Maybe Charlie didn't do this, maybe we blew a fuse or the bulbs just blew out."

He opened the panel up. There was not bulb one back there! Anyway, Charlie, we still love you.

Well we thought we would have a chance to get Charlie back. He had a beautiful chrome muffler on his bus, or a tailpipe or something. Benny said, "Boy, I really like that muffler. I sure would like to have one of those for our bus."

At the time we had a drummer by the name of Jimmy Johnston, and he was crazy. He said, "Well hell, get me a pair of pliers or a screwdriver and I'll get us one."

Of course, we would have given it back because it was a pretty expensive tailpipe. Anyway Benny handed Jim the screwdriver and the pliers, and Jim was under there working on it when Charlie walked up.

Charlie said, "Hey, what y'all doing under there?"

So Jimmy had a quick comeback and said, "Charlie, this tailpipe looked loose, so I just was tightening it up for you."

# CHAPTER ELEVEN

# BOYS IN THE BAND

You know I'm always surprised when an artist doesn't even know the names of the musicians who work with them. I was never a big star or anything, but I always made it a point to know my musicians and know their families and things. I think this benefits me more than them, because I got to know a lot of great musicians and a lot of nice families. Let me tell you something, friends: for all you would-be pickers, would-be singers, or whatever, if you've got musicians, and if you've got a band, get to know them and their families, get to know what they are all about. I think you will find it very rewarding.

We have had a lot of great times with our musicians, who have been real friends to us. We lived with them for all practical purposes. We have a lot of road stories.

Jimmy Fox and Sally Lorden worked for us for four or five years. Sally played bass and Jimmy played lead guitar. Some of the funniest times on the road were with these two people. At the time these things that happened, I didn't think they were funny. But, as I look back, they were hilarious. Deep down, these two people hated each other's guts.

One night we were in Florida and Jimmy's sister-in-law was there. She told Jimmy, "I watched that girl, and the whole time you were onstage she just stared at you. I think she's in love with you."

So anyway Jimmy was telling me and Benny all about this, and we all started laughing.

Benny said, "You dumbass, she is thinking of some way to kill you."

Early one morning, Benny had been driving all night and he was going to let Jimmy drive for a couple of hours. Remember this, our bus was eleven and a half feet tall. Well me and Benny laid down for an hour or so. Later we woke up, and people are yelling and honking. We heard this commotion and wondered what in the world is going on. Benny got up and went to the front of the bus. We was near Indianapolis, Indiana, and Jimmy had come to this tunnel which was only seven and a half feet tall. Sally kept saying to him, "You can make it."

Traffic was backed up quite a ways. Benny got behind the wheel and turned the bus around and got us out of there. But I think that Jimmy would have tried to go through that tunnel.

One time we was in Toronto, Canada, at the Horseshoe Club for a show. We was up on the stage with Sally playing bass, Jimmy on lead guitar, and Benny playing rhythm. All of a sudden Jimmy's guitar dropped out, and all he could hear was Benny and Sally.

Jimmy looked over at Sally with his fist doubled up ready to hit her, saying, "You tell her to leave my damn amp alone."

She was trying to adjust the amp the way she liked it.

Sally was a character in herself. At that time Jimmy and Benny dressed alike, and Sally's outfit was coordinated with mine. She wore a short black skirt and looked like the lady on *The Munsters* TV show. She made the statement one day that she wanted her dress short. This was about the time of the mini-skirt era.

I said, "Sally, if it was any shorter, people could see your underpants."

Well she said, "I don't wear any underpants!"

I told her that she is going to have to start wearing underpants. She went to the Woolworth store and bought some for nineteen cents each. She would wear them and then throw them away.

We were working in Virginia on the back of a flatbed truck. Sally would never drink water. Her skin was as white as chalk. She did not drink water because she said it poisoned her. We was working this show and I heard this clunk, clunk, and clunk across the bed of the truck. I turned around and a bee was chasing her all over the stage.

She was saying, "Get out of here you SOB!" at the bee, and it was coming out over the speakers. I was so embarrassed that I wanted to get under the truck!

I was having nerve problems so my doctor talked me into seeing a psychiatrist.

He told me, "I don't think you are crazy. But I want you to talk to this lady." So I went to see this counselor, and after a couple of sessions she told me there is nothing wrong with me, "but this lady Sally has got to go."

So a few months later I had to let her go. I have to say that deep down she was a great bass player and we had a lot of fun.

We would talk about her personal life and I thought, Oh my God, she has no morals at all. But I loved her anyway.

One day in Pennsylvania, Jimmy had picked up some woman and went home with her. So the next day we were at a country music park and had a two o'clock show.  About ten minutes till, Sally said, "Where's Jimmy?"

Benny said, "We can do the show, no problem."

Well about five minutes later, we saw this small plane circle around and around.  It landed in the big field by us, and here comes Jimmy with his shaving kit.  He wanted a raise because he couldn't get by on his pay.

Benny said, "No, you can't make it by chartering American Airlines to fly you around."

Sally had a seven- or eight-year-old daughter living with her sister in Chicago. She had just got home from going to Chicago to see her daughter, and her sister called and said to come back right away to Chicago. There was something going on that had to do with custody; Sally's sister had custody of the little girl. So Sally got back into her car after driving all day, and she headed back there. Well on her way, she was killed in a head-on collision. I felt really sad to hear that. Me and Benny was on the road when we called home and found out that Sally had gotten killed.

Sally was a very fine bass player. She learned from Buddy Emmons. Buddy was a steel guitar player, and his bass playing was secondary; but he taught Sally, and he was a good teacher because she was great. She was a good musician. She didn't sing no harmony when we first hired her. But me and Benny – we sang harmony, and we taught her to sing some harmony.

———

A lot of the musicians who worked with us have passed away: Danny Spinks, a very fine steel guitar man; Danny Tyack, a very young man who also was a very fine steel guitar player. BJ Wright lived in Gallatin, Tennessee, and he played bass and sang for me. He just died about two years ago. BJ was one of the finest singers that I have ever heard in my life, who never had a chance to do anything, but a really fine singer.

I just lost a piano player about a year ago, Robert Crigger; he'd been with me thirty-one years. He went overseas with me several times. Just a great honky-tonk piano player. We're still in touch with his kids.

We found out that Jimmy Stewart, who played drums with us, died here not too long ago. We had to read it in the union book; nobody told us. He had been buried before we knew it. It really upsets me, because we were pretty close to those guys.

Jimmy was one of our first drummers, back in the late '50s and '60s. Jimmy had a really bad drinking problem. He worked for a couple of years and then left us. He was an excellent drummer. He played on a lot of our sessions.

I remember one road story during Jimmy's time. We worked probably forty or fifty days for a gentleman named John Kelch. They were a bunch of telephone-sponsored shows. It started up in Maine and we worked through to California.

Well our guys started playing basketball. They were all in pretty good shape. I went and got me a whistle and a striped shirt because I was the referee. But I had to play one day. Jimmy Stewart had big long arms like an ape. He was guarding me and he kept swinging those arms.

I told him, "Get out of my way, or I'm going to bite you."

So he called a foul on me. "Foul! Foul! Foul!" he said.

Jimmy had a bad drinking problem and he knew it, and we knew it. We kind of worked on it together. His wife came out one night with Jimmy. Her name is Martha. He was drunk and she was drunk. They got into the damnedest argument that you have ever heard.

I told her, "Martha, go home." But she just kept on yapping.

I said, "Martha, go home." She just kept on.

I said, "Martha, go home, or I am going to kick your ass."

I was very blunt with her; I said, "Go home." She looked at me and she got real calm after that.

————

One night we were about ready to leave town but our drummer just didn't show up. It got to be midnight. We needed a drummer. So we went by Jimmy Stewart's house; but he wouldn't answer the door.

Well John Walker and Ray Emmett went around and had to crawl through his bathroom window. Jimmy was passed out. They got him up, packed a couple changes of clothes, found his shaving kit and his coat. It was really cold; I guess it was about fifteen degrees, you know; it was really, really cold. They wrapped him up in his coat, brought him out and threw him up in a bunk on the bus, and so we finally got on our way. We were going to Florida.

The next morning we stopped to eat. By this time Jimmy had sobered up. We had gotten off the bus, and he was still on the bus. We was watching out the window and saw him get off the bus. He had on this big, heavy peacoat, and he looked around – it was about ninety degrees, and he had this big overcoat on – he didn't know where he was. It was so funny.

————

One town we played during that trip was in a dry county in Alabama. They had a deputy sheriff who told Jimmy that he would get him something to drink. (But let me say that Jimmy always did his job onstage.)

Well the deputy went out and got him a big cup of vodka or something and sat it right down on the side of the stage. Boy, Jim was just frothing at the mouth trying to get to that liquor. When we got through with the show, I started to get off the stage, and I accidentally kicked that liquor over and it spilled out. Well Jim just sat down and cried.

————

Down through the years, I have had a bunch of characters in my band. One bunch that comes to my mind are John Walker, who played guitar; Ray Emmett, who played the bass and fronted the show; Dwight McClain on drums; and a gentleman named Jerry Day who played steel guitar. None of these guys were overly great musicians, but when they would work it would all come together and it was good.

John Walker was probably one of the damnedest characters that you could ever meet. You never knew when he was telling the truth. But we loved him to death. He was good for our show and such a good showman. John and Ray were very lively on the stage.

One night Ray Emmett, who was fronting the show, was singing a song called "Together Again." There was a bunch of young ladies down in front of the bandstand. John and Ray would try to impress these girls. So anyway John stepped up to sing the chorus of "Together Again" to harmonize with Emmett. Well John had false teeth, and as he stepped up to the mike, he sang, "Together—" and his upper plate come out about two inches. He was scrambling to get his teeth back in – it was so funny.

One time we was working down in Alabama. We had an afternoon and evening show. We done the first show and was going to get on the bus and go into town. We were a little ways out, so we wanted to find a restaurant to eat our supper. The bar person in this place was a lady. Well John loved the women, I tell you. So we asked him if he was going to town with us, and he said, "No, I think I'm going to stick right here."

She was giving him free drinks. So we went into town and ate.

When we come back a couple hours later you could tell that John was a little tipsy, but he wasn't too bad. The guys never got too drunk that they couldn't do their job; they really didn't.

We were on the stage, and into the show about fifteen minutes, and it come time for John to take his turnaround in the song. There was nothing; he wasn't even there. I turned around and wondered what was going on. I looked over, and saw that John had gone to the back of the stage and was leaning over the back railing, upchucking. Right there before God and everybody. I thought, "Oh my God, if I ever get out of here, I'll kill him."

Now these days you have a lot to contend with; and heavy drugs are involved in the entertainment business. I don't know much about drugs at all. But thirty or forty years ago, there was a little pill they called "old yellers." The brand name was Semco, I think. Then there was a pill about the size of an aspirin and it was yellow all over. Another pill had a pink side and a speckled side. So they called them "speckled birds." They weren't really dangerous unless you took a lot of them. Our guys would take them when they had to drive.

John Walker knew this place down in Alabama, and one time he told Benny, "Let's go down to Alabama. I know this place you can get this diet pill, these speckled birds."

So Benny said okay. When he came back and told this story, I didn't think it was the truth. He told it in front of John, and John just stood there and laughed, so I knew it was the truth. They went to this little place that was like a Dairy Queen. John drove up to the window and a lady came up to the window and said, "Can I help you?"

He said, "Yeah, I want a hundred speckled birds and a hundred Semcos."

He paid for them right at this drive-in window. Now this is getting a little loose, you know.

She said, "What name do you want them under?"

Well we had a little white poodle that traveled with us. His name was Pepé LePew. Since my married name is Birchfield, John said, "Put them under the name of Pepé Birchfield." So they bought pills under that dog's name!

Now John, at the time, was married, but was running around with this lady here in Nashville. She bought him a gorgeous necklace or a bracelet, I can't remember which it was. It was eighteen-carat gold and very, very nice. I knew that she had given it to him, but it was none of my business, you know.

Well about a week or two later, John's wife called me and she asked, "Where did Benny get that bracelet that he bought John?"

I said, "I really don't know."

She said, "Well I want to get him a necklace to match." She was trying to find out where he got it.

But I just said, "I really don't know, you'll have to talk to Benny about it."

Yes, John was quite the lady's man. Or at least he thought he was. I have a lot of fond memories of John. He died of a heart attack. When he had the first attack, we went to the hospital to see him. He asked us to pray for him, which we did. I thought this was really going to be a turnaround in John's life, but I don't know if it was or not

As I said before, Ray Emmett was a guy who was a real character. He wanted to be a star so bad. He done a good job, and sang just as good as a lot of them do nowadays.

Ray told me one time, he said, "I'll tell you what, I know a hit song when I hear it."

I said, "Really? You can pick a hit song?"

He said, "I can pick a hit song."

I said, "I tell you what I'm going to do. I'm going to set you up in an office and I want you to listen to all these songs, and you pick the ones that are hits. I'll give you a thousand dollars for every one that you pick that's a hit. But, if you miss, you've got to give me a hundred."

He said, "Oh, hell no." That put a stop to that.

Ray had some wife problems. We lived on the lake in Hendersonville and he come out to the house one day. About thirty minutes later, here comes his wife. They got in an awful fight right in my backyard. I thought, My God. He never did hit her, but she beat him up one side of that hill and down the other. I mean she was slapping and hitting and clawing and screaming at him.

After about an hour, I'd had it. I didn't want to do it, but I called the sheriff's office. They wouldn't come out because we lived in that little inlet out there that belonged to the City of Hendersonville. I like to never got the police out there and it got really bad; I was so embarrassed.

Finally I called the police and said, "If somebody doesn't come out here, I'm going to shoot these people. They won't leave."

Then his wife called us one night and said that the neighbor had shot him. So it scared us to death. Benny went down to the Memorial Hospital in Madison, and he told them that Ray worked with us. They said he was back there in one of those little rooms.

Benny went back there, and Ray was lying there on his stomach. They were picking buckshot out of his rear end.

Benny said, "Ray, are you okay? What happened?"

It had snowed and the yard was a little muddy. He said he was trying to move something for one of his daughters, or something like that. His truck slid over onto his neighbor's property and kind of left a little tire mark, you know, a little rut. So him and the neighbor got into it, and the neighbor went in the house and got his gun. Ray started running, and the neighbor shot him right in the rear end.

Ray told Benny, "I've got that son of a gun now; I've got him right where I want him. I've got him for shooting squirrels out of season."

———

We had a guy by the name of Dwight McClain who played drums. He had been a rock and roll drummer, and he was good. The first time he come out to our house to try out for playing drums, we saw him walking down the driveway – he had his breeches stuck down inside his cowboy boots. He thought that was the way you done it. A lot of people will remember an old cowboy movie star by the name of Hoot Gibson. He wore his pants stuck inside his boots. So instead of calling him Dwight, we called him Hoot.

Hoot fell in love everywhere he went. He'd meet a girl and fall in love, even though he was married. He ended up, I think, hauling three or four women back in U-Haul trailers to Nashville.

Back then we wouldn't take seconds to nobody on dressing. Our guys had five or six suits that Benny designed and had custom-made by his tailors in Hong Kong. They were beautiful. One suit, the pants were black with a red kick pleat on the side, and they wore a red shirt. Another suit had silver pants with a black kick pleat. They had blue pants with a white kick pleat on it. I mean they were beautiful. The one pair of pants they didn't like was the ones I did like. It was purple and white. So I made them wear them every once in a while.

Country pickers back thirty-five, forty years ago were the biggest bunch of characters in this world. We had this guy by the name of Jerry Day, an excellent steel guitar player, who went downtown one night and I guess he got to drinking.

Somebody said to him, "Jerry, who you working with?"

He said, "I'm working with Ronnie Milsap; who you working with?"

This guy said, "That's great, I'm working for Ronnie too." Of course Jerry didn't work for Ronnie, but he was just trying to play a big shot.

We were out in Arizona about forty years ago, and we played a club out there.  It was filled with American Indians. They were a great crowd. They had their own security force too.  As we were loading up to leave that night, a policemen told us, "You all better get out of here and don't stop for nothing. When these people get drunk, they do funny things."

When he saw us to the bus, he repeated it. "Don't stop for anybody or anything."

So we got back out on Highway 66. In a little bit, we was driving along and Benny said, "Look at that."

We saw this big Indian guy standing up alongside of the road, and he had something in his hands. He threw it over into the ditch.

I said to Benny, "We might ought to stop."

Benny said, "I'm not stopping for nothing."

What was this thing he threw over into the ditch? That really bothered me for a long time, and it has been forty years.

But you wouldn't believe some of the characters that have worked with us. There were so many great people: there was Bobby Bugg, who was a drummer; and Jimmy Johnston was a very good drummer, and we are still very good friends.  He is driving the bus for Rascal Flatts now.

Jimmy was Benny's relief driver. One time in St. Louis, Jimmy Johnston was driving, and he needed to back the bus up. He put it in reverse and backed it into the world's tallest building. He said, "Well I couldn't see it." Benny said, "It's the world's tallest building." It was something else.

He was a good driver, but sometimes he didn't pay attention or something. He took over to drive one day, and we pulled out onto this street and he hit a culvert. I was sitting in this seat that had a television set above me, and it hit me right in the head and nearly broke my neck. He just laughed, you know, and I thought, You son of a buck, I ought to throw this television at you.

I had some real to-dos with these guys. This bunch was so crazy. Let me tell you what they done. They got a pair of ladies' underpants and they put it in Jimmy Johnston's suitcase. He got home, and his wife found them. Well the next trip they ended up in Jim Whittaker's suitcase. He almost got a divorce. Then they ended up in Jerry Day's suitcase. They made the whole round. We went home one time, and I found them in Benny's suitcase. But I knew about them, so it was so funny.

Of course everybody knew Pepé, our little dog, who traveled a million miles with us. He was a very unique dog. He wouldn't have anything to do with you if you weren't a musician. If you were a musician, he would just love on you and let you pet him. But if you weren't, he wouldn't have anything to do with you.

Then we had this dog called Freckles. We lived on the lake, and Freckles could get mean. She was half German Shepherd and half Collie. All we would have to do was say, "It's okay Freckles," and she would just go on her way. She did not like Dwight McClain who played hard rock. This one time he come down to the house when they were fixing the road. John Walker, Ray Emmett, and Benny were down by the lake fishing off the dock.

Benny said, "Come on down, Hoot."

Hoot said, "I will if Freckles will let me." She had gotten between him and them. He'd go to the left, and she would go to the left, he'd go to the right, and she'd go to the right. She just kept watching and she wouldn't let him by, until we told her it was okay.

We had a Shetland Sheepdog named Fiddle. He was a gorgeous dog. I went to England for a couple of weeks. At that time we probably had six or eight dogs. I called home and Benny told me that Fiddle had died. It was summertime, and he went to the place where it was the coolest and laid down. He must have had a heart attack. His legs had just gave out and he laid on his belly. He just died there.

While we were up in Pennsylvania with Jim and Mary Custer, and we were walking around in this big shopping center, they paged me to go to the pet shop. Corey, who was four or five years, had saw this Shetland Sheepdog. Corey sat right down and said, "Now you just wait because my mama is going to buy you and I'm going to take you home." Of course we did.

———

I want to try to list all the musicians who worked for me at some point during the last forty years or so. I'm about ninety-nine percent sure that I got most of them, but if I missed someone I do apologize. I love all you guys!

Steel Guitar:

Bucky Baxter, Chick Beakley, Sonny Burnette, Jerry Day, Donnie Dion, Wayne Hobbs, Phil Koontz, Joe McGuffie, Jerry Merhar, Sonny Purdun, Danny Spinks, Danny Tyack, Big Jim Webb, Jimmy Yates

Lead Guitar:

Steve Bozeman, JT Corenflos, Jimmy Fox, Steve Hill, Randy James, Tommy Jones, Larry Nutter, Eddie Payne, Jackie Phelps, Gary Tinsley, John Walker, Stan Walker, Horace Whidby, Steve Wariner, Marty Stuart

Bass:

Larry Barnes, Ronnie Blackwell, Clayton Claxton, Danny Davis, Ray Emmett, Tommy Holt, Rick Langston, Jack Leonard, Steve Logan, Sally Lorden, Dick McVey, Randy Parton, Jim Whittaker, and BJ Wright

Piano:

Roger Guffey, Robert Crigger

Fiddle:

Leon Bolinger, Terry Morris, and Danny Parks

Drums:

Bobby Bugg, Bubba Heard, Jerry Ray Johnson, Jimmy Johnston, Lauren Lindsey, Shane McCauley, Dwight McClain, Bill Ryan, and Don Wainwright

I'm trying to think of all of these guys, but it's hard to, down through the years, since 1965. From the first time I formed a band to now, I've probably had a hundred musicians. I know I can't remember all of them. We have had a bunch of guys; our guys were great.

The guys I have now are Glen Dickerson on lead guitar, who is one of the finest guitar players to come to Nashville; he's been with me over twenty years now. Of course Benny plays the rhythm guitar; Rick Francis on bass, he's kind of the baby of the group. Rick is very quiet, but very funny, and one of the nicest people that you would ever want to meet. Dave Robbins is a very fine steel guitar player; he has been with me over twenty years. And Gregg Hutchins, my drummer, has been with me over fifteen years. Gregg is such a pleasure to be around. He is a second generation *Opry* musician, which is rare. His father Ray was The Willis Brothers' bass player in the mid-'60s. These guys are the only band I'll ever have with me.

# CHAPTER TWELVE

# COUNTRY MUSIC HALL OF FAME

I've enjoyed talking to you about a few of the people I've known in this thrilling business. It is a joy to talk about them. Things are different now, and in some ways that's a shame. The country music community has changed so much. I respect the younger musicians who love traditional country. Watching them making their own mark, I'm happy for them. Their road's just not the road I would take.

Unfortunately, I can tell you, many performers have been on the *Opry* stage the past few years who aren't even fans, who don't even know their roots. Several years ago Jan Howard was in the makeup room back here with some little girl who was getting ready to go on the *Grand Ole Opry*. Jan was making conversation, trying to get to know her a little; she said to the girl, "I guess you're a big Kitty Wells fan." The girl said, "Who's Kitty Wells?" She sure knew a lot about country music. If it weren't for Kitty Wells, that little girl wouldn't have had a place to stand.

To me the *Grand Ole Opry* is still a thrill. *It's still a thrill* to go on the stage of the *Grand Ole Opry*. Especially when you're with people like The Whites, or Steve Wariner, or The Grascals. There's so much praise to be given to the people who've come along later.

Even now, I am a fan. I'm very much a fan. I'm a fan of The Whites and Jan Howard and Jeannie Seely – these are my people. I love them and I appreciate what they've done for country music. Much of what they've done they'll never get credit for.

But the way music has been turned into a product has been a terrible loss. When Stonewall Jackson, with no contract and nobody knew him, could drive into town in his pickup truck and sing for the Solemn Ole Judge, George D. Hay, at WSM and then be put on the *Grand Ole Opry*, just because he was a good country singer – those days are far gone. Now it can be too much about marketing. I honor the giants of our music, like Lefty Frizzell or Kitty Wells. These are the men and women others try to imitate. They were the ones who set the standard. Others could only try to learn how to do it like they done it. They're legends for a reason. If it hadn't been for Lefty, many big country stars of today wouldn't be around. I know some who will credit him; George Jones did, Merle Haggard will, my friend Bob Luman said Lefty was his idol as he got started. As far as I am concerned, all of them learned something from Lefty. I wonder if the business bigwigs recognize what it took to make a country artist of that stature.

There are plenty of performers, and even plenty who make it to the stage of the *Opry*, but just making it onstage doesn't make you.

There's something you have. I don't think I'd call it greatness. For one thing, it is determination. It's something you build up over the years. Some people last a few years. I've lasted a lifetime.

One night backstage here at the *Opry*, Porter walked by me wearing one of his beautiful suits. Little Jimmy Dickens was with him and was wearing a sparkly Nudie suit too. Some younger group of musicians – I don't even know who they were – were standing around when they passed by. These boys kinda laughed. And one made a wisecrack, "Man if we stay around here long enough we'll end up wearing one of them suits." I turned around and said, "Son don't worry, you'll never be here that long."

The critical element is soul. What a real country music legend has in him that sets him apart from other artists, it's hard to put into words; but he's true to his music. I see it in Vince Gill, I see it in Steve Wariner; they're great musicians and songwriters. And they have sincerity. And they don't have to be told what to do. You just go out there and you do what you do. They like what they do and they do what they like.

Mac Wiseman and Skeeter Davis. If I got to pick two people to add to the Hall of Fame right now, they'd be my first picks; because they deserve it more than anybody else. Mac Wiseman's been in the business sixty years. I could name you twenty people that need to be in there. The Browns. The Wilburn Brothers. Jack Greene – he's got a great voice and a good history behind him. There are so many legendary country music people who have not been inducted into the Country Music Hall of Fame. Certain names are passed over, and then certain others are honored who cannot be called country. Or, very often, someone is honored decades late. I've told you some of those stories, people like Charlie Louvin. So the timing is off, to say the least.

There's always a lot of speculation about who has the final say. Who has the influence, and why? I believe it needs to be questioned.

In my case, they were about twenty years overdue. I just at some point decided they'd forgotten about me, and I forgot about them. And yet the time came when the CMA let me know they were inducting me. The day they called, for me personally it couldn't have been worse timing.

It was in late summer, 2011. It seems like it was a Tuesday. And it was one of the worst days of my life. My dear sister Quita had passed away. We just lost her the day before. The Hall of Fame was the last thing on earth that mattered. I had just lost my best friend.

There is no way to tell you how very close my sister Quita was to me. We had been through everything, all our lives.

I told them it was a bad time. I was grateful; it was a wonderful thrill. But I couldn't enjoy it. I was so hurt about Quita, it left me blah.

But there were ceremonies, there was the press, there were interviews. All I could do was rise to the occasion. It's just that I had no feeling for it. I wasn't there emotionally.

I remember at the press conference announcing the 2011 Hall of Fame inductees, I was up there with the MCs, Brooks and Dunn. While they was talking to me, Kix Brooks said, "Who was your idol more or less?" And I told him Kitty Wells. And he kept talking, and he kept on asking the same question. I said, "Kitty Wells." "Kitty Wells." "Kitty Wells." Finally he got it.

Kitty Wells – she will always be the Queen of Country Music. And not only that, she was just a precious, precious person. Beautiful. There's so much to be said about Kitty Wells. She had a heart of gold. Kitty and I kinda came along at the same time. I met her in California when her big record "It Wasn't God Who Made Honky Tonk Angels" was just bursting the country music industry wide open. I remember talking to Kitty and she was very elusive; I thought maybe she was stuck up. But boy was I wrong. She was without a doubt one of the sweetest ladies that God has put on this earth.

It is hard to talk about Kitty. We became very good friends the last five or six years she lived. The last few tours she worked, we worked with her. What a great career this lady had for sixty years or better.  We worked not long ago in Canada with Kitty, her husband Johnnie, and their son, Bobby. When she walked out on the stage, the people gave her a standing ovation, and rightfully so.

I remember one night, Johnnie was onstage talking about the women of the *Opry*; I was standing backstage. It was a show in Canada. And I ran out there and kissed him right on the mouth, and run back off stage. Kitty got so tickled. She just laughed. She said, "That's the funniest thing I ever saw."

Of course I've always been close to her. But I got real close to her in the last years. I remember while I was with her at Johnnie's funeral in September of 2011. She and I were standing there. He was laid out, you know. She said, "*Oh my goodness*, there's my singing partner." It was so sweet. I asked her, "Can I kiss him?" She said, "Why that would thrill him to death." Kitty only lived another nine months without Johnnie.

Words cannot express what Kitty Wells meant to country music. She made country music what it is. Kitty was there first. And I was thrilled to be right behind her. There was something about Kitty that just touched you; she was such a precious, warm-hearted person. There will never be but one Queen of Country Music; and you and I know who the queen is. May she reign forever. I love you, Kitty.

———

You know, her husband was half of the duo with Jack Anglin. There has been a lot of duets in country music, but nobody could ever equal the style of Johnnie and Jack. They had a unique sound of their own: kind of like a calypso sound. I got to know Jack Anglin fairly well before he was killed. He was on the way to Patsy Cline's funeral in 1963 when he had a car accident that killed him.

I loved Johnnie and Jack's music, and I still love them. Why are they not in the Hall of Fame? Even in his last performances, Johnnie Wright was just as lively as ever in his nineties. Johnnie, I love you, I love you, I love you my friend.

What a tremendous asset Johnnie and Jack's music has been to the industry: it was different, and it was a style that nobody could copy. The first few notes that they hit, and started singing, you knew who it was. To me that is what makes all the older artists in our business great. You could hear a Marty Robbins song start; just a few notes, and you knew it was Marty.

But the Hall of Fame skips certain legendary artists. Who knows why? They have been doing it for years: waiting until way past time (or never) before they recognize some of the influential figures; choosing less foundational people before them. I know how I got in. Bill Anderson and Vince Gill. They had a big part in my getting into the Hall of Fame.

I could tell you stories of so many legendary people whose induction was long delayed.

But one of the people longest delayed was Patsy Montana. She was the first female in country music to sell a million records. I think it was in 1936. When did they put her in the Country Music Hall of Fame? 1996! It should have been forty years earlier. She would have been the first woman inducted. What a shame it wasn't done before she passed away; it would have been such a thrill for her. My mother used to sing a song to me and it went like this:

> Love me now while I am living,
> Do not wait till I'm gone;
> And then chisel it in marble,
> Warm love words on ice-cold stone.

Patsy, I am sorry you couldn't have been here to enjoy what you have meant to the music industry.

Patsy's first hit song was "I Want to Be a Cowboy's Sweetheart," which she wrote. She did some yodeling on it. I yodel a little bit and this impressed me even though I was only six years old when I heard it. But as I grew older and got into the music business, I of course became aware of who Patsy Montana was. She had a long, successful career. I met and worked with her on several occasions. She was such a sweet, sweet lady. And she played the part; she dressed in her cowgirl suit and hat and cowboy boots, and it fit her to a T.

You know yodeling is really a lost art. In 1963 when I came out with "Second Fiddle," and I yodel on it, it got a lot of radio play. Patsy got in touch with me and she said, "You have made people aware that yodeling is an art that has almost been forgotten." She said, "Thank you for bringing it back to the forefront."

I told her, "You shoulda been in the Hall of Fame years ago." But she was so sweet, she wouldn't say nothing.

There are performers right now like The Whites who clearly have earned the honor of Hall of Fame status, and I hope they will be added while they are young enough to enjoy it.

Another early country music legend who is still yet to be honored: the Maddox Brothers and Rose. Rose Maddox was singing with her brothers when I lived in California. In later years she went more or less solo; her brother Cal would play guitar for her. One of my regrets is never following through with something I had in mind doing: I had plans to talk with Kitty Wells and Rose about the three of us going to cut an album together. The title of the album was going to be *In the Beginning* because we were the only three women that had any early prominence, so to speak. But we never did get it done. There is an old saying, my friend: Never put off until tomorrow what you can do today. It is so true. We put it off, and put it off, and it just never did happen. I am so sorry that it didn't.

The Maddox Brothers and Rose had quite a family. Their mother, Ma Maddox, was the manager for years. She was quite a character. She would have on black slacks, brown shoes, red socks, a green sweater, and an orange coat. There was nothing about Ma Maddox that was coordinated. But they made a lot of money.

There's a story about Ma Maddox going to a Cadillac dealership in Los Angeles. Because of the way she was dressed, all the salesmen had seen her and ran. But this one young man decided to ask if he could help her. She said that she wanted four Cadillacs and a Chevrolet.

He said, "Really. How do you want those financed?"

She said, "Ain't gonna finance, I'm gonna pay cash."

She had a cigar box under her arm and she doled out twenty-five or thirty thousand dollars in hundred-dollar bills. She got Fred and Cal and Rose and Henry a Cadillac, and she bought Don a Chevy. He was about twenty-four. She said he was too young for a Cadillac.

I went up to see the Maddoxes perform at the Happy Go Lucky Ballroom in Tulare, California, one night. I went to see everybody I could see, because I just loved the music so much. Cal played rhythm guitar, and he had this real silly laugh that he did. They was playing their music and Ma Maddox walked up, crooked her finger and motioned Cal to come over to her. He walked over to her and bent down, and she slapped him so hard it sounded like a gun going off. He never lost the smile on his face or anything. I was standing right there and I heard her say, "If you do that again, I'll send you back to the cotton patch where I gotcha."

I think Rose contributed a lot to the ladies in country music. Later on after singing with her brothers she cut an album with Buck Owens. So I think the devil needs to give her her due. I love you, Rosy.

She was hard to get along with; they just didn't, for some reason or another, make friends easy. One time she said, "Ain't none of you women can sing a song like it oughta be sung. Y'all just try to copy me."

One time Rose came to the *Opry* here, this was probably forty years ago or so. She just walked in one night. I was about the only person she knew.

I said to her, "Hey, Rose, you want to sing one of my songs? I'll give you one of my songs." At that time you'd get two songs on the *Opry*.

She couldn't get over it. I went to Hal Durham, who was the manager at that time, and I said, "Rose Maddox is going to sing my second song." So my guys rehearsed with her. By doing that, it sealed our friendship. She just couldn't get over anybody doing that, you know, giving up a spot so she could sing.

We were over in Austria in '97 and she was trying to remember the words to "Loose Talk," a song that she and I both had recorded. It was a Freddie Hart song. She just couldn't think of the last verse. Well I tried to tell her what the last verse was, and she just got really pushed out of shape.

> They say you are leaving that you are deceiving,
> But you tell me they say the same about me.
> But we'll show them they're wrong, that loose talk will do harm,
> And hope that the truth they will see.

She said, "Oh, Jean, you don't know what you are talking about. That's not right."

I said, "Okay, sing it your way."

So she kept fooling around with it, rehearsing it, and finally, it come to her what the last verse was.

She apologized and said, "You're right, you're right."

Rose was already sick then. She came home and went into a nursing home in Oregon. I called her every three or four weeks. I knew she was sick. I called one night from the *Opry* to tell Rose I was going to dedicate her a song. The nurse said, "Oh Ms. Shepard, you just don't know how much it means for you to call her. She gets so beside herself, she is so grateful, you know, that you called to check on her."

Some guy who had a little recording studio in Austria sent me a record not long ago that he made me. It was a recording of me and Rose while we were on that Austria trip, singing "The Unclouded Day" in his studio. He had recorded her singing the first couple verses, "O they tell me of a home where no storm clouds rise...," and then I came in and sang two verses. I was with Brian Skylar, a Canadian country music artist; we've worked together a lot these later years. He sang harmony with Rose and me on the chorus. It was just this little room, this studio was; but he had top-of-the-line equipment. I had forgotten about the recording. He sent it to me about three months or so ago, and I put it on my stereo, and I said, "That is one of the best-cut records I have ever heard."

I don't think people in country music give the Maddox Brothers and Rose their fair dues. They think there's no place for them, that they're too hillbilly. Bull.

———

Skeeter Davis was a lady who should have been in the Hall of Fame years ago, but if it's ever going to happen she is not here to enjoy it. Skeeter was one of us, and the minute she opened her mouth you knew who she was. She had old country harmony that was wonderful. In the later years, Skeeter had so many country classics. She became not only a national star, but an international star as well. She had hits in the pop field that went gold. People loved her wherever she went.

I considered Skeeter one of my best friends. She joined the Opry in in 1959. We both traveled with Ernest Tubb a lot. We just loved to talk. We got together and just talked non-stop. Ernest loved to take pictures and he used to put captions under these pictures. One day we were waiting on his bus and we were both sitting in one seat. I was sitting across the arm and we were both talking when Ernest took our picture. A week or so later, he showed us the picture and his caption under the picture was, "Who Is Listening?"

Skeeter lost her fight with cancer ten years ago. She had a lot of trials and tribulations throughout her life. She was strong in her faith in the Lord, and her faith stayed strong until the end of her life. I remember that every time I saw her perform, all I could think of was, More! More! She proved that she was a trooper, from the word Go. I will always miss her.

———

Here's a man I saved for the last to talk about. I think the last time I ever talked to my dear friend Ken Nelson was at the time they announced his induction to the Hall of Fame. By that time Ken was almost ninety. This was in 2001, seven years before his death.

I called him. I said, "It's about time." He said, "Oh well sweetheart, don't worry about it." It didn't bother him. But it bothered me; because he was such a good person.

Ken was the last of the big producers to be elected to the Hall of

Fame. He wasn't part of the Nashville clique. By that time the CMA was getting its foot in the door and spoiling the whole process. Ken didn't play politics with Nashville, and that's why they passed over him so long. Nobody told me that, but I believe it; because I know how Nashville is.

Ken produced the first-ever live album of a country artist. It was Hank Thompson, *Live at the Golden Nugget* (1961).

He was a great producer. Ken would always tell the musicians, "This is Jean's session. Everybody remember that." And if anybody got too much, he'd tell them.

Back then you'd find a sound that fit an artist. On my records, Ken would put a lead guitar and a steel guitar together. And that was my sound. Ken created my sound. Everybody had a sound. When a disc jockey played a record, you knew within the first few notes who was going to sing that song. The moment you heard the first notes, you'd know: that's going to be Faron Young, or that's going to be Marty Robbins, or whoever. That's what the great producers did. It was that way for years. But you hear a new country song, you have to wait till it's half over before you know who is singing.

Back in the '50s, '60s – I wouldn't trade anything for my memories. What made it so good, you commented to each other: "I heard your song the other day...," and you were truthful; you'd tell them what you thought of their new song. You supported each other. Now it seems like if one of them gets a hit, don't none of them back it. Back then, we was for one another. Shoot fire, if Skeeter had a hit I was thrilled. We were family.

Our time has been here, and it's gone. And I guess that's the way it should be. I can't believe it's gone. I watched the trends change and I thought for a while we could save it. But country music won't never come back to what it was. The country music they play today is not country music, and that's what hurts me. These youngsters come out onstage with their screaming guitars and loud, banging drums. The *Grand Ole Opry* doesn't need that.

Country music is country music. You can't paint it no other color. I got to be there during its golden age, right in the middle of all of it. It was glorious.

I just did what I wanted to do. I thank my parents for that, and the good Lord. People have said I broke ground as a solo woman singer. They said I paved the way for the next ones – Loretta, Tammy, Dottie, and them – in the days when female artists used to always come as part of a family act or a duet. It wasn't a conscious thing. I'm just a strong-willed person, and I used the gifts I was given and the confidence my parents installed in me. They backed me. Mother wasn't necessarily happy to see me go into the music business but she backed me fully, because she knew that was what I wanted to do. I loved it. I did what came natural, and the Lord made a way I guess. Me, Kitty Wells, Rose – people group us together whenever they go back over the history of country music. It was just a man's world. And we were the few women. There wasn't no one for us to follow, no women. But I didn't set my mind to make history. I don't believe they did, either. We just saw what was the obvious thing for us. It fit us, so we pursued it with heart and soul and strength. It's the way you get anything done. If you love it, do it.

I'm proud to know my career did my fellow female artists good. I think it shows: Do what you're meant to do. Go out there and give it a try. We all have a role, and you never have any idea how you are going to affect your world. You're given certain gifts. I hope everyone reading this will take my mother's advice. I wanted to sing. I knew I could sing a good country song. Mother said if you don't have confidence in yourself, why would anyone else? So I sang. And here I am. Still singing.

# ENDNOTE FROM JEAN

There are so many great, touching stories that people don't know about country music entertainers. I am so glad that I can share a few of them. The people that I am writing about in this book are truly the greatest in country music. They will always be the ones that put it on the map and pushed the door open for generations to come. Some of these memories have never been told. I cherish these memories. I hope that everybody will read them and know they come from a loving heart.

Having the friendship of all these wonderful people has meant more to me than the words can ever start to tell. I'm sure there are some artists I have overlooked. When you try to recall friendships over fifty years, you are bound to overlook somebody. So please forgive me if I have overlooked anyone.

I hope all of you have read this book with an open mind. Believe me, nothing that I have said was intended to cause any hard feelings or to hurt anybody in any way. I lived through ninety percent of these stories, so I know that they are true.

If you have enjoyed my stories in this book, I would recommend you order the Country's Family Reunion videos made possible by Larry Black. They feature some of the entertainers of country music who are no longer here, and these videos would be a treasure to have.

My Mother told me that if I don't have confidence in myself, how did I expect anyone else to.

It was probably the best advice I ever had – from a lady who only had an eighth grade education. After that, I planted my feet on solid ground and told myself that I know I can be what I want to be. I knew music was what I wanted to do. I had a taste of the music industry and this was where my heart was.

I have remembered Mother's words for the last 60 years. I tell anybody who comes and asks for advice. I tell them exactly what my mother told me.

# SPECIAL PEOPLE

Here are a few select people who, although I mentioned their names within the pages of my book, have meant much more to me behind the scenes. I just have to set aside this section to acknowledge them.

To start off with, I can't think of anybody better than Kitty and Smiley Wilson. They recorded on several of my records with me. Their daughter, Rita Faye, did too. Smiley and Kitty were wonderful, wonderful people, and their contribution to country music should never go unnoticed. They recorded with Ferlin Husky and the Duke of Paducah, among others.

Kitty Wilson was always telling tales. She's kinda like me, a very straightforward, unpredictable person. She said she got on the bus one day with the Duke of Paducah and they was working with the Carter family. I loved Helen, but she always had something wrong with her. She got on the bus and said, "Oh, Kitty, my stomach just hurts so bad, I wonder what in the world is the matter with me?"

Kitty said, "Oh hell, just go to the back of the bus and fart, and you'll be okay."

But that was just Kitty Wilson. Smiley would just look at her and say, "Good God almighty, Kitty." He just couldn't get over her. But they were wonderful people. Later on, Smiley became my booking agent. They are both gone now, but I loved them dearly.

————

I have special gratitude toward my older sister, LaQuita Alexander, who helped me remember our childhood and those special memories. She was so very precious to me. (LaQuita passed away in 2011, prior to this book being completed.)

————

I want to speak about a lady who has been with me right at forty years, and it is Kay Helfrich. She's from Ft. Wayne, Indiana. I met her years ago up at Buck Lake Ranch in Angola, Indiana. She and her sister would always bring food out to us. There were no restaurants or grocery stores around there anywhere, because it was out in the country, in this big park. She fed everybody from the Grand Ole Opry at one time or another: There was Billy Walker, Tex Ritter, the Drifting Cowboys – all the people from the Opry.

Kay come to work for me, gosh, I was pregnant with Corey, and that's been forty-three years. She is my hairdresser, my seamstress, my housekeeper, my secretary, my babysitter, my dog sitter, and my house sitter.

Everything that needed to be done, Kay helped do it. She has been a dear friend all these years. She raised Corey, our youngest son, from the time he was born, right on up to the present time (I am gonna say to her: Kay, you didn't do too good a job! No, I am just kidding.), and is still helping with some of my grandkids.

She has meant a lot to me and still does. She's kinda like me, she is getting old and decrepit, but Kay, that is what we get. I couldn't have done it without you. I love you, my dear.

————

I want to say something about Mari Hart who helped me start this book. We have been at it for quite a few years, and finally got it all together. I've known Mari since 1960 – good grief, Mari, you are not that old!

Mari is from Herkimer, New York. I don't remember where I met her, but I think it was at *The Friday Night Frolics* when the show was at the old WSM building in downtown Nashville on Seventh Avenue North. She was friends with me and Hawk back then, and was there with me through all the trials and tribulations. She was here when my first child, Don Robin, was born; and she showed up at the hospital. (I had to laugh the other day when Don Robin got his AARP card. And I thought, Lord of mercy, it doesn't seem like it has been that long.) She was there when my second baby, Harold, was born, and she was there when my third baby, Corey, was born.

One day she brought her dog, Dusty, out to my house. He was a golden cocker spaniel – a beautiful animal, and I loved him. He had passed away. She asked me if she could bury him out here on our farm. This really meant a lot to me. I said, "Yes, you can." So we buried him out there in our graveyard.

Down through the years, Mari has been there with me, and I have treasured her friendship. We have become very, very good friends, and I truly love her. I want her to know what she has meant to me.

Hopefully, Mari, this book will sell a million copies. I ain't counting on it, but we've had fun, haven't we?

> Knowing Jean all these years has been very special to me. She is a true friend who listens, advises, and laughs with me. She is like a sister who will help me no matter what. Thank you, Jean and Benny, for your wonderful friendship. I love you both!!
>
> Love, Mari Hart

---

Ruthie Mae Bauer – I would be remiss if I didn't mention my good friend, and she has been for the last twenty years or so. Ruthie Mae came up here from Florida, with her husband, Frank. She will never know how much she's meant to me through the years. She is constantly with me at the *Grand Ole Opry* and has taken so *many* pictures. A lot of the pictures are on the front of my last few CDs.

What a character! She is always buying me something. I tell her, "Don't buy me no more shoes, or don't buy me no more coats." But, she is a very kind, giving, and loving person. Ruthie is always there, ready to help out in any way that she can, and I truly love this lady. Ruthie Mae, I love you!!

> Jean, you have been my very dear friend these past twenty years. You bring so much joy and happiness to my life. What a thrill it has been, being with you at the *Grand Ole Opry* all of these years. You have made my life complete. I mean that with all of my heart. I thank you and Benny for making my long-time dreams come true.
>
> Your Sidekick, Ruth Bauer

Judy Mock has furnished some of the pictures for this book. Judy, I really thank you for your help. You have been a friend down through the years, and I appreciate and love you very much.

> It has been my privilege to take photos of Jean and other country music stars since the early '50s, and was considered a good friend to all of them.
>
> Judy Mock

———

And many thanks to Jim and Mary Custer, who were my fan club presidents for years. They always worked the Fan Fair and put up our fan club booth. One time, we won second place!

We stopped having a fan club years ago, but remained friends down through the years. They are from Camp Hill, Pennsylvania, where Jim was once a truck driver. Recently Jim passed away; now Mary's health isn't good, either. We still call her about once a month. When she says, "Didcha eat already?" we know it is Mary.

When we would go down to Florida, they would come to see us and usually spend a couple of weeks. Wonderful people – we have had some great times together. They traveled with us all over the world!

Mary, I love you all and I hope you enjoy the book.

———

I also thank Pam Preston, who took over the fan club after Jim and Mary. Pam is married now and lives in Gallatin, Tennessee.

Carl and Sally Niblett were, I guess you could say, our constant companions and traveled with us for about three years. They were funny and a fun-loving couple. One time in Canada we played this fair and Carl and Sally was with us. There was a huge crowd and they sold our products, you know, our CDs, tapes, pictures, and things.

Before the show, we rode around the fairgrounds and was looking for something to eat.

Sally said, "Well over there they've got some pootang."

Now if you are not from the country, and you don't know what pootang is – it is a nice way of saying "sex."

Well my mouth dropped open.

She said it was only two dollars.

Carl, her husband, said, "By damn, I got my two dollars."

I could not believe that she had said this. I said, "Sally, what did you say?"

She said, "They've got some pootang over there."

I was just stunned. I said, "Sally, do you know what you are saying?"

She said, "Yeah."

Carl, Benny, and me was just dying laughing. She was referring to poutine which is actually french fries with some gravy over them.

This was the funniest thing in the world. Every time I call her, I ask her if she had any poutine lately. She just cracks up. At the time this happened, we told her what it meant, and she said, "Oh my gosh." She had heard it somewhere, but she didn't know where.

———

Also I have had a bunch of wonderful fans that belonged to my fan club, too many to even mention. We have remained friends down through the last fifty years.

––––––––

Last but not least: Benjamin Howard Birchfield.

Benny has meant an awful lot to my career. He drove the bus for me, he played in the band – he done all that had to be done. Because he is such a good mechanic, he even worked on the bus. We have been married for some forty-five years. It's been a rough and tough road, but, Dad, we've made it despite everything. We made it!

––––––––

I hope you have enjoyed this part of the book because it has meant a lot to me to be able to say thanks to all my special people!

# ACKNOWLEDGEMENTS

*EDDIE STUBBS* – What can you say about Eddie Stubbs that hasn't been said?  He is a connoisseur of traditional country music.  I met him many years ago and we have been friends down through the years.  I truly admire Eddie and treasure his friendship.  I am glad you are on my side, Eddie, because you love country music as much as I do.  Thanks a lot!

———

*FORMER SENATOR STEVE FARIS* – Former Senator Faris is one of the finest men that I have ever had the pleasure of knowing.  I met him backstage at the *Grand Ole Opry* many years ago.  I know he has been a big fan of mine. He did a radio show out of Arkansas and has always made a big push for strictly traditional country music.  I love you, Steve, and I am so happy you are on my side.

*GUS ARRENDALE* - I met Gus through a cousin of his who happened to be my vet from Gallatin, Tennessee. Dr. Arrendale called me one day and said, "I've got a cousin coming in from Georgia who is in college. Do you think you could get him backstage?"

I said, "I can handle that."

This how I met Gus. He come in laughing and joking. That was about twenty years ago, and he has been a joy in my life; he really has. He is the president of Springer Mountain Farms chicken, which is out of Baldwin, Georgia. They elected me to be the spokesperson for their company. I have been with them for about the last fifteen years; and it has been a total joy working with Gus Arrendale, John Wright, and all the people there. They are the best people: very community-minded. The only thing I can say is that I sincerely love these people at Springer Mountain Farms – especially Gus, baby.

———

I want to say thanks to Ruth Bauer and Judy Mock for all their pictures in this book. Judy did the front cover and Ruth did the back cover. I want to mention and thank Curtis Hilbun who took the picture of me and Ruth.

———

Thanks, also, to my manager, Michael Souther for his help in proofreading this book.

I wanted to sit down and have a personal conversation with every reader of this book. Thanks again for all your help in making this happen.